17

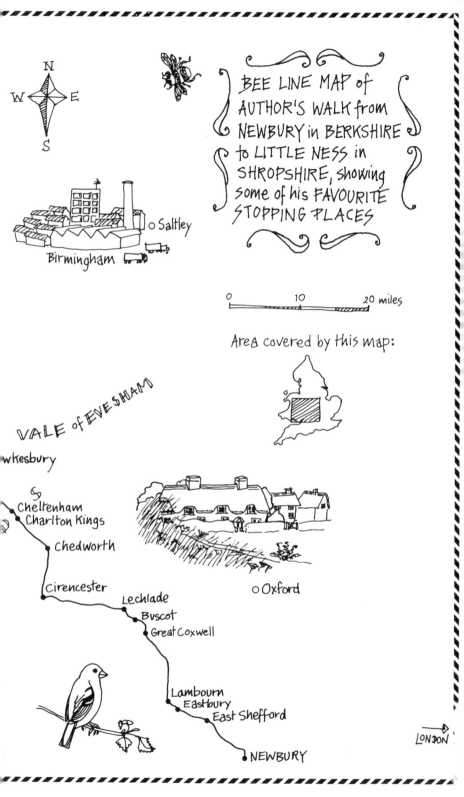

Oswestry
Llanrhaeadr
Sycharth
Baschurch
Llanfyllin
LITTLE NESS
Bwlch y cibau
Shrewsbury
Trefnanney
Annscroft
Welshpool
Hookagate
Acton Burnell
STIPERSTONES
Rorrington
Pulverbatch
LONG MYND
Norbury
WENLOCK EDGE
Bishop's Castle
BROWN CLEE
Ditton Priors
Clun
TITTERSTONE CLEE HILL
Cleeton St. Mary
Cleobury Mortimer
Ludlow
Clows Top
Stockton on Teme
Shelsley
Suckley
Cradley
MALVERNS
Mathon
Colwall
Hereford
Hollybush
BLACK MOUNTAINS
COTSWOL
Bristol

# PETER DAVIES

# THE FARMS OF HOME

WITH DRAWINGS BY SANDRA OAKINS

André Deutsch

First published 1993 by
André Deutsch Limited
105-106 Great Russell Street
London WC1B 3LJ

0 233 98838 6

Printed in Great Britain by
WBC, Bridgend

To Esther, with gratitude

*'. . . The church and yew*
*And farmhouse slept in a Sunday silentness.'*

Edward Thomas, 'The Manor Farm'

# CONTENTS

# PART ONE

# WHERE IT ALL BEGAN

# A Question of Sheep

'You can milk a cow – and you lived at the farm by the church.' The Vice-Principal smiled when he made this statement while interviewing me for a place at Saltley Teacher Training College, Birmingham, in April 1949. There was no question in his voice; no note of surprise, but one, possibly, of admiration. He seemed to be pleased and satisfied with that. He must have known that I could write English from my letter of application, clipped there on the desk before him with a solid testimonial from our old vicar: To Whom It May Concern. Nothing was said of my reasons for leaving farming; my short stay in London where I had a place at the Guildhall School of Music; my departure after only one lesson due to my inability to find somewhere to live; my leaving my gloves behind, which the tutor had to post on to my mother's new home in Shrewsbury, where she had said 'Typical!' – then asked me, casually, had I thought about becoming a teacher. There would never be any shortage of children, she pointed out, 'you can count on that!'

But there was nothing casual about this man, Mr – no, Major James Chance, M.C., T.D. In some remarkable way he made me feel special.

'You're offering history as well as English,' he added, again with a smile. 'Have you worked at any time with sheep?'

'Er, no, I'm afraid not,' I replied.

'Pity,' he said. 'Sheep, more than anything else, have made England what it is.'

Forty years on, I remembered those words, which is why this book came to be written.

3

'You are free to go to Chapel: you are not free to stay away.' Major Chance was being firm. The assembled one hundred and fifty men, mostly with their pullovers the wrong way round to conceal their tielessness, toyed with the cold beans left on their breakfast plates.

'Don't attempt to eat while I am speaking!' Forks slid back in place and arms nearly folded themselves. 'And I don't want to see any more scruffy heads and people improperly dressed on a Monday morning – or any other morning!' His knowing eye, enlarged by strong-lensed spectacles, rolled with the assurance of an old campaigner's. His steradent-aided smile added brilliance to the sharp edge of his remarks. Iron-grey and tall as the Duke of Wellington, he smoothed the slight crumpling of the unironed fringes of his gown. 'And the gate will be closed at nine instead of ten o'clock.'

Clank! We were just on the point of asking if we might have something for breakfast other than the 57 Varieties when he twirled his mortar-board and announced that the Principal had let it be known that he liked baked beans.

We shuffled disconsolately out to prepare for first lecture which was, ironically, Health Education. Major Osborne, the softer of the Physical Education teachers, talked about athlete's foot and prickly heat – two disorders of the flesh as far removed from my experience as any tropical disease.

'Ask him about blackheads,' whispered Bonzo from Scunthorpe.

'Or ingrowing toenails – mine's killing me in the gym,' piped Barnsley Bates. You could tell by their voices, if not by their names and faces, the geographical origins of Pacey and Robinson, Hadley and Bullivant, Rushton, Relton, Machin and Needs. Our year was made up mostly of level-headed Northerners with a strong sense of duty, smelling of soap and corduroy, and shiny withal. They came from Coalville and Leicester, Barnsley, Burnley, Burslem and Stoke. I seemed to be the only countryman there.

We all wore sensible shoes, grey or lovat-green trousers, or strong tobacco-brown cords. We sported Harris tweed jackets (no loud checks) and kept our hair in place. They (not I!) were organized and interested in organizing others. Many had teachers in their family; some were the sons of teachers who had trained at this very place. Most had done some teaching before coming to college. I was exceptional in that no member of my family had ever expressed any interest in becoming a teacher. I did not express much. And my scant interest in soccer marked me out.

My first visit to the common-room was a revelation to me. There was a woman wheeling around what looked like a lawnmower on a lead. I had never seen a vacuum cleaner before.

'She's hoovering,' someone explained.

In that same common-room, on Saturday afternoons, everyone huddled round the radio mesmerized by the voice that rose with a high score and fell with a low, or flattened out on a draw: 'Newcastle United, one; Manchester City (pause) three. Blackburn Rovers, two; Sheffield Wednesday, two.' The students were friendly, serious, natural, and, so far as I could gather, not given to books.

Short-haired and long-scarved, we moved about in neutral groups with biros and binders, snapping the *obiter dicta* of the staff.

It was a Spartan life for the first year. Each man had a

5

small bed in a corridor of corrugated cubicles, a 60-watt bulb, a small chest of drawers and a three-cornered wash-basin with one cold tap. Most of us were over twenty and one was thirty-three. Several had held high military rank.

Our grey Gothic building was lit with lancet windows and decorated inside with the universal post-war cream. What it would have looked like without its shiny, fresh-faced youth I could not imagine.

The architect of this society, the overlord, the Governor, to whom all questions – *exeats*, exceptions of any kind – were referred, was Major Chance. He it was who minded our affairs; down to what we should eat and what we should put on. The Vice-Principal of a small Church of England teacher training college is, I suppose, as important as the dean of a cathedral. He may even order the bishop about.

I did not know all this, of course, when I boarded a Number 8 tram in the centre of Birmingham (the first I had ever seen) and trundled uncertainly, swaying east to Nechells, past Lea and Perrins' red-brick factory lacquered in sauce, on to Alum Rock. My eyes began to smart, my tongue to go dry. My nose picked up the rank, corrosive smell of gas. Bad eggs! It was like the chemi-lab at school. Getting off the tram at College Road, I sniffed the air. But you could not call it air. The back of my throat was pricked by needles. There was no wind. I would die under this pall; and be buried. Cut off in my youth. One of the books in my bag was *Under the Greenwood Tree* – set for the English and Drama course I was about to take up.

Indoors, in the soon-to-be-familiar common-room, I fell in with an interesting lad who had a kind of half smile, half grimace on his face. He told me his name was Adcock and asked me mine. I said Peter. He said John.

'Unusual,' I said. He laughed. He had an odd way

of nearly closing his eyes when he laughed.

'It looks as if you need a sense of humour here,' he said, did a half turn and unveiled his eyes. They were blue and candid. I knew we should be friends.

'Lefty' Wright joined us, sticking out a nicotined paw, and, man of the world that he was, made us laugh with a joke which broke the ice all round. I heard it several times next day, spluttering round the corridors like a jerky Jumping Jack. Someone always missed the beginning, so he had to tell it again.

The college was one hundred years old; and in that time it had furnished itself with a music room (usually locked) with only one piano; a couple of common-rooms (first year, second year) with table-tennis tables, one pair; a chapel with an old organ, which, in the centenary year, quickly became a chapel with an organ that was new; a playing field; a tennis court; a gymnasium; a craft room; a visual-aids room and a library.

I frequented the library, large and Dewey decimalized. It was there that I discovered Wordsworth and transcendentalism. There, in a trance, one evening in October I forgot the suffocating air outside and went 'in heart and mind' to the banks of the River Wye to see:

> These hedge-rows, hardly hedge-rows, little lines
> Of sportive wood run wild: these pastoral farms,
> Green to the very door; and wreaths of smoke
> Sent up, in silence, from among the trees!

Here was I, fresh from the farm, 'in lonely rooms, and mid the din of towns and cities', sharing Wordsworth's recollections with him. 'Almost suspended, I became a living soul; my mind a mansion for all lovely forms.' Tears dropped on my paper as I wrote. It was after ten o'clock, lights out, before I was prised by the duty librarian from my work, and I worked on in my room with its 60-watt bulb. And on for several days.

I could not leave that essay alone. I polished it and polished it. I always handed my work in late. (I still write like that; I will not leave ill – or well – alone.)

Philip Dunn, my Eng. Lit. tutor, had set that essay, perhaps to see what imagination this sprig of youth had. He was easy-going, so I knew I could delay. I had a dozen disappointing drafts around my room, and was reluctant to let him have the one that was good. I parted with it almost in tears.

Bunny was my other English tutor – Burrow by name. He was like a Galapagos turtle: evolution had passed him by. He read 'The Elephant's Child' and *Paradise Lost* like a gramophone record. He had a cleft palate and sideways teeth which forced him to e-nun-ci-ate 'by the banks of the great, grey-green, greasy Limpopo river (all set about with fever trees)', the words driven up into the echo chambers of his desiccated head. He held the book not so much to help him read as to show off the moonstone ring on his right hand, which was reflected in the pin in his tie and the lustre of his light blue eye. He lapped one wing of his gown over the opposite forearm, creating the effect of an antique bird.

Bird or reptile, his breed is now extinct. He was an anachronism even in the feudal forties. But think on. . . . Hundreds of men must have read aloud 'The Elephant's Child' with him in mind, and thousands of children received a ghostly glint of those moonstones and the sideways teeth; an echo of that strangely mesmerizing, high-pitched voice.

Bunny, a bachelor, had rooms in the college and was

diligent at curfew time. 'Punc-til-i-ous', he would have said.

'Curfew, from the French, of course – *couvre-feu*: a safety measure, you see, gentlemen.'

Bird or reptile by day, he became a bat at night, winging through the vasty corridors and sounding out pockets of resistance around the changing rooms, the table-tennis areas, or the secretary's office where Davies and Adcock might be still printing one of their subversive news-sheets – 'po-ten-shially sub-versive, enn-y-way!' Following his peculiar echo-location system, he came calling: 'Come along, gentlemen – nearly ten o'clock – time we were all in bed.'

'Come along, John,' I would say. 'His Master's Voice!'


Perhaps I had an exaggerated idea of my own musical ability but I never regretted not taking music at college. The recorder was in vogue. The playing of this instrument by children is bad enough; in the hands of grown men, who are also learners, it is unendurable. Lefty, Adcock and I went to the cinema some evenings, driven from our studies by indifferent individuals who piped indifferent pieces indifferently, in different rooms. That was one frontier we could not cross. We went to Alum Rock, where we could usually find Humphrey Bogart or John Wayne, neither of whom would ever have held a recorder to his lips.

Lefty was a bit like Bogart. Hunched. Collar up. Back towards you, voice kept low. Lefty would sell you anything – a tip, a joke, an education textbook – for a fag.

Other absconders were Wallace and Pugh. They were theatre-mad. They went to *The Lady's Not for Burning* every night for as long as it ran, ditto *Death of a Salesman* and *A Streetcar Named Desire*. Their rooms were stuffed with 'props': hats, falsies, handbags, crimped hair for wigs, everything there ever was for *The Importance of Being Earnest*. There, grease-paint and spirit-gum ruled over gas.

And Relton – what shall I say about him? He went to the theatre, too, but to play in the band. I never heard anyone play the trumpet like him. I sometimes accompanied him on the piano. When we could get into the music room. . . .

There were many fine musicians at Saltley; and many fine actors. McCarthy was as authoritative in *Noah* as Donald Wolfit was in *King Lear*. 'Charge!' shouted Lapworth, in *Arsenic and Old Lace*, and acted everybody off the stage. 'O youth! The strength of it, the faith of it, the imagination of it!'

It was in drama and music that frontier posts stood open sometimes for the daring and the imaginative to cross. I lacked the strength and faith to play on the stage. Besides, I was too gauche. But neither did I keep to my books, as Finney did. Tan-eyed and inscrutable, Finney had a quiet confidence and consistency in performance that I could not match. I envied him his inner security, his outward self-control, his tidiness, his unimpetuosity. He did not waste time or energy. He did not go out every night, or punish himself in the gym.

It was very noticeable that first and second years at Saltley did not mix. There were no rules about this. It just wasn't done. The one field where the gate was wide open, of course, was that of sport. I was only a moderate athlete and gymnast; and in games where it was possible to predict the bounce of the ball I was frankly inept. My first love was rugger. So when Hardcastle pinned up lists on the notice-board of Possibles and Probables to play for the college and my name was among them my hopes ran high.

I was a wing-forward, competent enough for occasionally getting off-side in my eagerness to tackle the opposing scrum-half. But the long, dry summer of 1949 had left the pitches at Stechford where we played bone-hard. Twenty minutes into the game the scrum-half had fallen on my right hand and, small as he was, broken two of my fingers. I felt sick, not so much at the sight of blood as at their dismembered shapes. Hardcastle, the referee, leaned over me. He looked concerned. I grinned up, wincingly.

'Bad luck,' he said. McCarthy, who had been an officer in the Navy, offered to take me to Birmingham General Hospital in his little red 'bus': a Morris convertible, I think.

'Put my coat round you,' he said. 'You must keep warm.'

I was conscious enough to notice his confident handling of the car, but none of the landmarks on the way to the hospital. The most easily disorientated person on earth, I was absolutely lost in the vast, cream-coloured corridors of the General. I wasn't fit to be in a nursery-school team, I told myself, in a sudden rush of self-pity. McCarthy had given me some money to get the Number 8 tram back to college, but I didn't know where from and I felt cold, lonely and afraid. He had offered to wait for me; but I was glad he had gone. I might burst into tears.

Nurses, big and bolstering, bounced me out of myself; and I remember apologizing to the Staff for swearing under the anaesthetic.

'Sure, that's nothin',' she said. 'An' oi'm Oirish.' She even pointed me in the direction of Martineau Street and the tram.

My right arm in a sling and two fingers in plaster, I was an unworthy hero back at College – with a harvest of concessions: 'No need to take notes for the moment,' the lecturers said.

'I had to have gas . . . they strapped me down . . . they took a nail off or something . . . I swore blue murder,' I whispered into the tendrils of hair twined round Lefty's ear, he biting his nails with excitement. He would have given the nurse more to apologize for. He was a natural wide-boy, down to the tips of his stubby fingers fumbling his greasy, crinkled hair.

Every week I went down to the General. A terrible waste of time. But I still played the piano, with my third and fourth fingers cocked out of the way of Bach's exacting counterpoint.

'Praise me if you can, blame me if you must – but for God's sake don't ignore me.' Major Chance lecturing on child psychology was bent on not ignoring us.

Being a military man, he lived, not in a room like Bunny, but in his own quarters in the college grounds. He was, he let it be known, a student of character. He did not beat about the bush. He did not run round corridors. He was a still figure at the centre, the college revolving round him. He studied us from his observatory.

The 'rogues gallery' – the photographs of students behind the staff common-room door – provided him with faces on which to work. Thereafter came the filling in. He seemed to regard me as more than a country curiosity.

'Tudor,' he pulled me up one day. 'What do you know about Cobbett?' Others called me by my first name, but the Vice-Principal called me Tudor. He must have thought I was Welsh.

'Oh, *Rural Rides*!' I sang. And he, not staying for an answer, said 'Write me an essay on Cobbett.' The faith of the man! And me with my arm in a sling.

Emboldened by his confidence in me, I searched the library shelves. No *Rural Rides*. Only *Advice to Young Men*. I trembled as I opened it.

Back in my closet, I read the introduction. 'It is the

duty, and ought to be the pleasure of age and experience to warn and instruct youth, and come to the aid
of inexperience.' Then, in 'Advice to a Youth', Cobbett
says: 'Start, I beseech you, with a conviction firmly fixed
in your mind, that you have no right to live in this world;
that, being of hale body and sound mind, you have no right
to any earthly existence, without doing work of some sort
or other. . . .' Ah-ha! 'Dress should be suited to your rank
and station . . . be always as clean as your occupation will,
without inconvenience, permit . . . He who will not work
shall not eat. . . As to drunkenness and gluttony. . . .' I
was appalled. And enthralled. What a swaggerer he was,
this Cobbett!

Was it my own hard upbringing on the farm that drew
me to these eighteenth-century writers: Cobbett, Blake,
Arthur Young and Tom Paine, improvers all? The radical
in me was coming out. The puritan, too. They appalled
me one moment; they thrilled me the next.

'Hallelujah, I'm a bum!' my brother had written that
week from Western Canada. He was rounding up sheep
on the prairies, riding a pony western-style, shooting at
coyotes by day and sleeping in a bunkhouse at night. He
had left his job as a physicist at the National Research
Council in Ottawa, being worried that he was contributing
to the development of nuclear war. He was riding the box-
cars like that other Davies, W.H., a couple of generations
before. He, like W.H., had been challenged on the roof of
a freight train by the conductor whose job it was to knock
the hobos off with a stout iron bar. But John's biggest
worry had been when a train went through a tunnel with
no headroom to spare.

And here was I, cribbed in my cabin, with my Cobbett
on my knee; my chief concern, the manner in which I
should conduct myself.

'As to friends and acquaintances . . .' Cobbett darkly

13

warned. I liked to identify my friends among the types so broadly painted in his tract. '. . . and in this school I learned that men, fond of gaming, are very rarely, if ever, trustworthy.' Lefty was addicted to cribbage. 'This vice creeps on by very slow degrees. . . .' (everything, according to Cobbett, could become an ungovernable passion).

He also had a very poor view of recreation. 'Manage well your time,' he said; 'and to do this, you must have as much day-light and as little of the candle-light as is consistent with the due discharge of your duties.' Adcock never seemed to go to bed. 'When people get into the habit of sitting up merely for the purpose of talking, it is no easy matter to break themselves of it. . .'

He was downright scornful of looking-glasses. 'A looking-glass is a piece of furniture a great deal worse than useless. Looking at the face will not alter its shape or its colour; and, perhaps, of all wasted time, none is so foolishly wasted as that which is employed in surveying one's own face. . . .' I could see myself in this. But in my pictureless cell, my small shaving mirror was a singular indulgence indeed!

'I once heard Sir John Sinclair ask Mr Cochrane Johnstone whether he meaned to have a son of his (then a little boy) taught Latin. "No," said Mr Johnstone, "but I mean to do something a great deal better for him."

' "What is that?" said Sir John. "Why," said the other, "teach him to shave with cold water and without a glass." '

I put that story in the next news-sheet, and noted in my essay that I would have met with Mr Cochrane Johnstone's approval on both counts, having failed to learn Latin but succeeded many times, at home in Little Ness, in shaving under the pump.

Water was all a young man needed to drink, said Cobbett. Wine was out, and so were 'slops'. No cocoa then at supper time, made with dried or sterilized milk.

The water in my room tasted of tar.

I concluded my essay, left-handedly, with the thought that I admired the sound of Cobbett more than the sense; that, while Garrick trod the boards, our William had stumped all over England, France and America, the sky his sounding board; that we were lucky to live in England – I knew this would please the Vice-Principal – where men are like beetles in the grass; some, like Cobbett, climb to the top of a leaf (I wanted to say he was no end of a blade) very full of themselves, whence they shout down to the rest of us, telling us how it is done.

Once, in the spring of the year, we had a dance. The girls of Shenstone College came to us. Later in the year, we might go to them. This was an event that no one could miss. The notice-boards throbbed. Instruments, normally chaste and classical, snarled and scraped out 'In the Mood'. The corridors were invaded by scent. It was the time of *Oklahoma* when every lad looked like Curly, every lass his clear-eyed girl. The smell of the gasworks was abolished that night; nicotine gave way to after-shave. Lefty did not look like Bogart – more like Fred Astaire; Adcock less like a roving reporter, more like the Student Prince. Hardcastle was first onto the floor and into a quickstep with a girl who looked like Carmen Miranda. Relton captained the band. Tunes from *White Horse Inn* gave way to 'J'attendrai', 'La Mer', 'We'll Gather Lilacs', 'Always in My Heart'. . . . I could just manage a foxtrot – one, two three, four, PAUSE, now and again. My favourite was the 'Destiny Waltz'. Polkas brought me out in a sweat. And 'Jealousy' (the tango) brought me out in a rash. There were no drinks. And that was the trouble with the College Dance: you had to concentrate on your movements. You had to watch your step.

15

You could not take a girl to your room. There was no room! Even second-year students could not get away with that. A rumour that someone had hidden his girl in the wardrobe when suspicious friends burst in was spiced with the conclusion that she had had to come out because of the smell of his socks. The notice-board added a rider: DON'T KEEP YOUR SOCKS IN THE WARDROBE IF YOU WANT TO KEEP YOUR GIRL.

I met Madeleine from Much Wenlock. She was a cool, Deanna Durbin type of girl, like apple blossom in May. She waltzed me high in the clouds, and while we sat out the tango – too technical for me – we roved over Wenlock Edge. We talked of Clunton, Clungunford, Clunbury and Clun (ours were the quietest voices in the hall that night). In imagination we were married already, both teaching at some little two-teacher school.

The band was in shirt sleeves and summery hats. Relton was playing requests: 'Hear My Song, Violetta', and 'People Will Say We're in Love', 'Papa Niccolina', 'The Donkey's Serenade'. I asked Madeleine what songs she liked.

'Over the Rainbow – and Gracie Fields singing the Lord's Prayer,' she smiled. Would I request 'Over the Rainbow', for her, please.

Her eyes were misty with delight. I decided they were hazel, not brown; her hair dark chestnut, not brunette. She was so compact and neat; her simple white dress suited her perfectly.

'Where troubles melt like lemon drops . . .' she sang in a small pure voice. Her lips and teeth were shiny-moist, as were her eyes and even her little ears, their beauty enhanced, as all delicate things are, by moisturizing: a spider's web, a fingernail, a pebble by the sea. . . .

I was just examining her nearer ear when Elphick, our visual aids wunderkind, appeared. He was wearing a white laboratory coat with the sleeves rolled up. He whispered something in my ear.

'Aren't you dancing?' I asked – my mind momentarily disengaged.

'No, I've been processing a film in the dark room.'

'Out of the dark, and into the light!' I smiled.

'You're wanted on the phone.'

'The phone?' I said.

'The phone,' he repeated. I was holding up a busy man. I shrugged and smiled at Madeleine who said she'd keep my seat.

I think there was only one phone in the college. Certainly, there was only one that I ever used. And I only used that once. Phones were associated with running across two fields to call the vet from our old kiosk by the church. They were associated with desperation and death. I picked up the receiver uncertainly.

'Hello,' I said.

'Is that you, Peeder?' an unfamiliar voice enquired. 'It's Jan.'

'Jan who?' I asked.

'Your brother John. I'm calling from home. Mother's ill.'

The voice sounded American and strange. I could not believe it was my brother's. I nearly put the phone down.

'Mother ill?' I asked. 'What do you mean?'

'Very ill,' the voice said. 'Likely she won't live. Can you come home?'

'Yes – I suppose I can. Yes – I'll—'

'You'd best come first thing tomorrow—'

The line went dead. The penny dropped inside my head. I hadn't heard from Mother for about three weeks. We were near the end of term. I knew I'd be going home. But I had been out of touch. Anything could have happened to her in three weeks. I would have to go home – home that was not home any more. I went outside for air. The

17

cold moon hung directly over the Vice-Principal's house.
The clock at the Rosary Church struck ten. Some lines of
Housman came into my head:

> *The farms of home lie lost in even,*
> *I see far off the steeple stand;*
> *West and away from here to heaven*
> *Still is the land.*

> *There if I go no girl will greet me,*
> *No comrade hollo from the hill,*
> *No dog run down the yard to meet me:*
> *The land is still.*

The air outside was warm round the hall. There was
even the scent of mown grass on the playing field. I
badly wanted to be in the athletics team next term. What
if I had to leave? I went indoors. I heard the booming of
the band. Good night Irene, good night Irene, I'll see you
in my dreams. . . . That must be the last waltz, I thought.
Who might be partnering Madeleine? I did not look in to
see, but made my way up darkened stairs to my room.
Mine must have been the only 60-watt bulb alight in all
those empty cubicles when I took off my clothes and went
to bed.

'Good night ladies, good night ladies . . .' echoed across
the quad.

I spent a desolate Easter at home. Mother lay listless in a
private nursing home. (She had always been too proud to
pay her stamp and shunned the N.H.S. imagining, rightly
or wrongly, that she was not entitled to use it.) She was
heavily drugged with streptomycin, unable to read – partly,
perhaps, because she was unable to sit up. I did not realize

18

that she had, in effect, given up this life; that she was a shadow, a ghost, taking no further part.

I had a Penguin book of stories by D.H. Lawrence, from which I read her 'The Woman and the Gipsy'. It turned to ashes in my mouth. I took her fresh salmon for tea. She lay unmoved, her head turned away, her thoughts behind unseeing eyes a thousand miles away.

All her married life our mother had wanted a house with a tap. For twenty-five years she had lived in the old malthouse at Little Ness – Church House, as we called it – where oil lamps smoked and candles dripped and water came from an outside pump. Now she had taken a 'thirties house in town. But the little watch whose noisy ticking had regulated all our lives, finding itself in a bijou box, fell silent. The doctors listened. The spring was gone.

Summer flowed on. Back at college, the second-year students were getting rid of their books – something that did not bring tears to their eyes. Their assessments were over, applications for jobs had gone in, and books were up for sale: all the education textbooks, the Nunns and Valentines and Jeffreys; the *Silent Social Revolutions* and that well-worn realm of last resorts, *Backwardness in the Basic Subjects* by Fred J. Schonell. A copy of *Tess* or *Lord Jim*, most popular of set-books, could not be had. McCarthy only had *Youth* left. And he gave it to me.

'If you get a really rotten class on your first Senior Practice, read *Youth*.' He meant a really rotten Secondary Modern class.

I had served my time with the infants at Loxton Street. ('You have to be able to do their buttons and shoe-laces up,' said the head.) I had battled at Bordesley Green with forty juniors in my class. ('Davies would be happy in

19

chaos,' said my tutor for P.E.) Now it was time for me to face my first Senior Practice. It was well known that steaming twelve-year-olds, in the great City pent in June, did not take kindly to stew-pots offering them enlightenment. Shades of the prison-house began to close. . . .

At St Thomas's R.C. Secondary School all the teachers carried canes. The headmaster stayed in his study which they, the teachers, called the Ivory Tower. I was prepared for hell.

I was given a bunch of backward boys for English, last period in the afternoon, twice a week. There weren't many of them but they were so inarticulate they found their greatest happiness in shuffling their desks around. Even as they sat, a desk would come shunting towards me on a trial run – forwards, backwards, sideways chassés. . . I told their class-teacher: 'They're not backward. They've got four forward gears and a reverse!'

Both the class teacher and my tutor had suggested that they should write something, a letter perhaps. Scott, the pack-leader, gave out the paper, stopping to talk to his friends on the way. He was, in contrast to the scruffy majority, fresh-faced and clean around the ears. He had watchful, penetrating blue eyes – the only hard feature in an otherwise girlish face.

'Right,' I said at last. 'Pretend you are on holiday – on a farm or by the sea.' Outraged appeals from Scott. The pack shunted in amazement. 'Now, write a letter home,' I went on. 'I'll help you to begin.'

'My Dear Parents,' I wrote on the blackboard.

'That's not what I call'm,' said one.

'Hey, me nib's broke,' said another.

'I am writing to tell you what an exciting time I am having. . .' I persevered.

'Never 'ad an 'oliday,' they repined. 'Never seen the sea.'

I looked at my words on the blackboard. They lacked

conviction to my eye. The writing was not good. But somehow by pressing on I hoped that they would share my zeal. Commitment might be catching. By turning round I might become confused.... 'What an exciting time!' I read it through. I'd started something. I had got them going. Could I get them back?

'Right.' (I always said 'Right' when things were going wrong.) 'I'll read you a story.' ('Read us a sto-ree!') 'A tough story. Life at sea. Told by a man who really knew what it was like.'

'Yes,' I began reading Conrad's *Youth*, 'I have seen a little of the Eastern seas; but what I remember best is my first voyage there. You fellows know.... You fight, work, sweat, nearly kill yourself, sometimes do kill yourself to accomplish something – and you can't. Not from any fault of yours. You simply can do nothing, neither great nor little – not a thing in the world – not even marry an old maid, or get a wretched 600 ton cargo of coal to its destination.'

I noticed a smile at the mention of the old maid. They put themselves in first gear, shunted once more, then listened.

In the ten minutes left of that lesson, I got them aboard the *Judea*, with Marlow and the bandy-legged skipper, Captain Beard (who didn't care for writing) and – cutting short the sixteen-day journey from London to the Tyne, and Mrs Beard with a face like a wrinkled and ruddy winter apple – we got straight on with the collision, the captain adrift in a boat without oars, the three weeks' delay, the Channel run, the storm and the failure of the pumps.

'We pumped,' I went on, immersed in the drama of the tale, 'all night, all day, all the week – watch and watch. We forgot the day of the week, the name of the month, what year it was... We had forgotten how it felt to be dry.

21

'And there was somewhere in me the thought; by Jove! this is the deuce of an adventure – something you read about.'

The class teacher came in. 'You've got them,' he said. 'The bell went, and you didn't even hear it.'

'Just a bit more,' I said.

'I would not have given up the experience for worlds. Whenever the old dismantled craft pitched heavily with her counter high in the air, she seemed to throw up, like an appeal, like a defiance, like a cry to the clouds without mercy, the words written on her stern: Judea, London. Do or Die.'

'*Youth*?' said the class teacher. 'Conrad, eh? Well, fancy that! Scott's dad was a sailor – went down in the war.' He looked at his watch. 'I'm on last duty – I'll have to go, old boy,' and he picked up his cane to go out. 'Don't worry about the writing – or lack of it. Pump something into them first. Empty vessels make the least sense!'

And as he went the class filed out, reluctantly, it seemed.

'What's an anagram of schoolmasters?'

'Cart-horses.'

'Too many r's; not enough letters.'

Adcock and I were assembling the first copy of our new weekly magazine: *The Saltette*. When ready, I would take it down to the Vice-Principal.

Further down the corridor, Finney was making a cool dissection of *The Insect Play*. Two doors down the other way, Bates, four foot four in his socks, was standing on a chair giving his familiar recital of 'The Volunteer Organist': 'The organ and the organeest – who volunteered to play!' He always sang it soulfully, unaccompanied, straight. No one ever knew if he was serious or not. We laughed and applauded and patted his back. He did it as if in a trance. Perhaps he was a medium – a small channel of grace.

Fairbrother said he was glad when it was over. He could concentrate on his Time Line. We all did a time line. I had a piece of paper with the Romans, the Normans, the Mediaevals, and Us on it. But Fairbrother's was actually illuminated. I mean it had bulbs, wires and switches. It had Gothic lettering. It filled his room and took up all his time. It was the Time Line to end all time lines.

In the Craft Block puppeteers were puppeting and potters were pottering. In the visual-aids Room skinny-armed Elphick was unwinding and rewinding ticker-tape miles of film; myopic and pink behind tortoiseshell specs, he synchronized his spinning spools like night-jars churring in the dark.

In the gym, P.E. specialists were hanging in crucifixes upside-down on the wall bars. One or two were doing hand-springs on the buck and pommelling the pommel-horse. Only Hardcastle was stretching his hamstrings on the floor. Yet we all knew that when it came to a gymnastics display his hand-springs would be slower, higher and more poised than anyone's.

I knocked on the V-P's door. He called me Tudor, as usual, and asked me in. He had, on the mantelpiece, a very nice piece of pottery called 'Breasting the Storm'; a man – it might have been a shepherd – leaning into the wind. I judiciously admired it while he looked unseeing through *The Saltette*. It would be all right, he signalled, handing it back to me.

'Who's paying for the paper?'

'Oh, we will. We have adverts, and we charge tuppence a copy.'

'Will I have to pay?'

'Yes, sir; I'm afraid so.'

'I shall look forward to some good film reviews. Are

23

you going to The Rock tonight?'

I knew that he knew. And he knew that I knew that he knew.

Once in a hundred years we had a really interesting visitor. Memorably, in 1950, it was the Archbishop of Canterbury. He came to our centenary: an animated little chessman, rigorously robed for his duties. Relaxed, gnomic and gaitered, he threw a leg over the corner of a common-room table and looked and talked like Charles Lamb. He had that extra clear enunciation that certain people with prominent incisors have. He spotted my *Saltette* and took it up with vivacity.

'This is the thing,' he said: 'plough the field but don't neglect the headlands! All the wild things of the hedgerow – the little by-the-bys.' We timid flakes of manhood began to snowball round him. We thought we had captured a leprechaun. Half-seated on the edge of the table, informally swinging one leg, he parried our attempts to pin him down. He twinkled like a tiddlywink. He shifted his ground as often as he readjusted his seat. He regaled us with stories of Repton where he had been head. His famous family. His views on Church Unity. I had a curate friend whose wife believed passionately that the Anglican Church was endowed with the true Apostolic Succession. I asked him what he thought of that idea.

'Like the curate's egg,' he said. 'Good in parts.' He chuckled and swung the other leg.

'How does the wealth of the Church square with Christ's teaching in the Sermon on the Mount?' Lefty asked.

'Render unto Caesar the things which are Caesar's. . .' His eyes twinkled over the top of his glasses and he slapped a ringed hand down on his knee. 'That's my text for the service in the morning. I'll answer you then.'

'Aren't all the best hymns by Methodists?' asked Adcock, who must have been one of them.

'And Anglo-Catholics,' he replied. 'Praise to the Holiest in the Height!'

The mention of Catholics reminded me of Cobbett who attributed all our nation's misfortunes to the Reformation. I could remember his words in *Advice to Young Men*.

Cobbett, I pointed out, mounted an astonishing attack on the Protestant record and the lying historians who had, he said, supported it.

'That was one of his hobby-horses,' said the good Dr Fisher. 'He rode it for all it was worth. And that wasn't much,' he added.

There was no unseating this little man. With a quick readjustment of the clerical buttock, he squatted on the other half, turning, as it were, the other cheek.

He sounded us out, getting at our interests, our accomplishments.

'You are an intelligent/talented/well-informed lot!' he egged us on. His ability to keep the common touch and his capacity for mirth must have helped to keep him young. The common-room provided us with common ground. How many times, I wondered, in one hundred years, had a great Christian teacher sat like this among the young?

Finally Adcock bowled him the googly, long held back.

'Religion is largely wishful thinking,' he said.

'What's wrong with being wishful? What's wrong with thinking?' the Archbishop said. 'High is our calling, Friend!' And as a parting shot he suggested that 'for homework' we might like to strike out of the epistles every mention of hope. 'What would be left?' he asked.

'Faith and charity,' Adcock conceded.

'Exactly,' he said.

Mention of homework and epistles put the cat among

the pigeons and we all unwillingly dispersed.

I went back to my room and marked the boys' letters. Most of them had written nothing more than I had written on the blackboard. Some had written Dear Mum and Dad. One had written Dear Mum. From the writing, I knew it was Scott.

Back at St Thomas's the following Tuesday, I went on reading *Youth*. 'Boys, the house on deck is gone . . . let's look for the cook. . . . There he was, sitting in his bunk, surrounded by foam and wreckage, jabbering cheerfully to himself. . . We snatched him up, lugged him aft, and pitched him head-first down the cabin companion. Those below would pick him up at the bottom of the stairs all right. We were in a hurry to go back to the pumps. That business could not wait. A bad leak is an inhuman thing.'

Forced back to Falmouth, our young storyteller still dreamed of Bangkok. 'Meantime,' as he says, 'the owner, the underwriters, and the charterers squabbled among themselves in London, and our pay went on. . . Pass the bottle.

'Then, on a fine, moonlight night, all the rats left the ship.'

The regularity of that hypnotic cadence, 'Pass the bottle', the seaman's diction, the jeering boys and the long-shore loafers: 'She'll never get to Bangkok!' held them. And the smell as if 'paraffin lamps had been flaring and smoking in that hole for days. The cargo was on fire.'

'Go on, sir!' Nobody called you sir on teaching practice. 'Stew-pot', yes. But sir was reserved for senior staff. Like the deputy head who told us not to joke with the kids. 'I never told a joke in class till I'd been here five years,' he said.

'Next day,' I went on, 'she began to smoke in earnest.' Those empty vessels of mine were soaking up sense. They listened even while I departed from the text to tell them about Falmouth, Bangkok, Australia; cargoes and steam-ships, and any general knowledge we could dredge up between us.

It became apparent from my questioning that Conrad was right: the sea enters into the life of most men; they know something or everything about the sea, in the way of amusement, of travel, or of bread-winning. He seems to have known intuitively what was good for boys. He would have enjoyed hearing me catechizing those cane-hardened Catholics between bouts of his burning adventure. Their only movement was to sniff imaginary smoke, smile and put heads down on folded arms.

'Now, if she only would spring a tidy leak – it would put a stopper to this fire. Wouldn't it? . . . Do you remember the rats?'

'Sometimes a man, as he dashed a bucketful of water down the hatchway, would yell out, "Hurrah for Bang-kok," and the rest laughed. But generally we were taciturn and serious – and thirsty. Oh! how thirsty! And we had to be careful with the water. Strict allowance. The ship smoked, the sun blazed. . . Pass the bottle.'

When I finished the book, Scott came up to me.

'Sir, can I borrow that book?'

'Borrow it, Scott? I'll give it to you!'

Hurrah for Bangkok! Hurrah for Youth!

Fair as Adonis, Scott smiled his thanks and farewell. He, like all his classmates, seemed curiously vulnerable in the end: caned every day, it must have come as a relief when Conrad dealt them a blow to the head.

Shelley made wings for other people to fly on, someone

said. And Conrad, the alien, picked out a cinder from the smouldering cargo of the *Judea* and lit – how many? – fires in Youth.

Soon, all too soon, exams were over and job applications sent out. There was only my assessment to come. Whatever my tutors thought of me, I thought very highly of them. Steadily, year after unremarkable year – with only once in a hundred years a visitor as distinguished as the Archbishop – they pleaded the causes of 'The Elephant's Child', baked beans, hard work and fair play.

And one gave me a Big Idea. To walk back to the Farm by the Church.

# PART TWO

# TRUDGING

# I take to the open road

Training, tunnelling, triumphing and – if you are lucky –
time for amendment of life: that is the ordinary teacher's
lot.

The training takes two or three years (some post-war
students did it in one and they were among the best that
ever entered the service).

The tunnelling takes thirty to forty years, a period
in which you either lose your way underground and
see no light at all, or more felicitously swim underwater,
catching refracted images of the world above and around
you – there being but little lower than you.

The triumphing comes when you retire, and lasts about
a day.

It's the 'time for amendment of life' that interests me.
It is when the shades lengthen, the busy world is hushed,
the fever of life is over and our work is done. . . . It is
like the sunset flight of the dragonfly. The hard part is
over: the two years in the mud, the seemingly interminable
struggle to find your wings, manouevre them, then find a
wife. The rest is easy for the dragonfly (we think but do
not know – Nature sometimes stamps a Monty Python
foot).

I suffered many a set-back in my dragonfly career. I
was too bold, too innovative and erratic in my flight. I
was thought to have a big head. I certainly did not try
to hide the colour of my wings. I flew too near to the
sun. I was cast down. But I had nerve and imagination, as
Major Chance must have spotted in that awkward imago –
I will not say nymph – not yet fully formed in 1949. Forty
years on, Wordsworth's 'glad animal movements' still not
beyond my powers, I felt 'a presence that disturbs me with
the joy of elevated thoughts'.

31

I remembered and accepted the Major's proposition that sheep, more than anything else, had made England what it is. I would go in search of the golden fleece, and, like Wordsworth, I would walk.

It was with this idea in mind that I planned, in March 1990, a walk of about two hundred miles through some of the most beautiful parts of Britain, all famous for sheep, to see for myself how they had left their mark on the landscape, influencing our architecture and the very fabric of our society.

I saw that if I walked from my present home near Newbury, to my old home at Little Ness, I would be following a more or less direct north-westerly route, over the Downs, the Cotswolds, the Malverns, the South Shropshire and Welsh border hills. I drew a bee-line map, bought a cheap pair of Czechoslovakian boots, dusted off an old haversack and set off.

'Gorbachev, Gorbachev!' shouted our thrush from the birch tree by the gate, 'Pick 'em up!' A collared dove teased me with his 'Bravo Titch!' and a chaffinch chipped at a tune which might be rendered 'In the pink!' Which was how I felt as I headed up the sheep field, the wind butting my back. That wind had been getting up like a mad ghost all the year, and seemed to have been associated with wild-eyed moons. It would help me to navigate: while it came at my back, as it did, from the south-east, I would know I was heading north-west. 'Bravo Wind!'

If ever a town's prosperity was founded on wool, Newbury's was, so I should really have started from there. Instead I thought about it as I walked down the valley road towards Rood House, remembering how a window in the Church of St Nicholas is dedicated to the memory of John Smalwode, alias Winchcombe, 'to whose munificence the erection of the church is mainly due'. The high and nave altars, says the guidebook, are newly dressed with plain all-season Laudian frontals of wool and 'in keeping with the appropriate traditions of a church built largely from the proceeds of the ancient woollen industry in the area, a fleece from the locally bred Romney Marsh sheep was incorporated into the yarn.' Once, in the interval of a concert in that church, I could not resist running a fold of a frontal between thumb and forefinger, and fine wool it is.

But why a Romney Marsh sheep? And where, on this first morning of spring, were the traditional Hampshire and Oxford Down sheep? They were not in our sheep field, nor were any of the eight hundred odd Mules, the Blue-faced Leicesters crossed with hardy hill breeds that make up the bulk of commercial flocks now. They were all in the lambing sheds, not due to drop their singles, twins or triplets for another week or so.

Rood House was asleep. Even the goal posts on the playing fields looked sleepy as I headed down the valley road. I say 'down' because, I suppose, the sloping shoulders of our valley are so high and the early descent to Welford is so steep, you hardly realize you are going upstream.

This indeed is one of the most beautiful parts of our valley. It is emerald, it is jade; it is green with green willow; and what is that, at this time of the year, but gold? Grey wagtail flickered by Welford bridge; and they were not grey, but yellow and blue. The river, the Lambourn, wandered off into a multiplicity of channels, as it threaded its way to the Kennet at Newbury. The land round here – especially on a spring morning, sodden with dew – is like a sponge. These are the old water-meadows that have not been drowned and drained and drawn for hay for many a year. They were showing their age through neglect. Not to mention the hedges, which, like me, were roving free.

At East Shefford I came to a bend in the river, trees on either side of the road haunted by rooks, what looked like an island with swans, and perhaps the most splendidly sited house in the whole valley, the Mill. A house set among trees is always enhanced, like a beautiful woman's face framed by hair.

There must have been many millers along this rich valley; more than one in most villages, driving – nay, grinding – hard bargains, especially in the nineteenth century before the Corn Laws were repealed.

Great Shefford Manor, the first of my 'farms by the church', was asleep. The round, honey-pot tower of the church peered over its mossy dovecote and roadside barns. About the fifth century A.D. invaders from the continent penetrated this far up the Kennet and Lambourn. They married native British women, apparently, for only a small minority of the female skeletons dug up behind the Manor here (some by Lambourn Valley Railway work-men in 1890) showed the physical characteristics of the invading type. Teutonic tribes, especially Saxons, practised cremation. These wives, our local archaeologist, Mr H. J. E. Peake, concluded, were Christian and may have persuaded the new society to adopt their Christian burial customs. A ford, a farm, a church: how much history slept under their stones.

I ran up the hill, light-footed invader that I was, and now there suddenly were sheep: not Hampshire Down, not Oxford Down, but all sorts of sheep, down by the river on my right: Jacobs and Herdwicks and some that looked like goats – *were* goats! A sanctuary perhaps for refugees? And donkeys and ponies, geese and swans, all in a happy confraternity down by the water's edge.

34

The hedges here were low and leafing out with light
green 'bread-and-cheese'. I picked a piece, soft and tasty
for breakfast, the freshest thing on earth.

I passed East Garston, cradled in the valley to my
right, and came panting to Eastbury. Panting not with
tiredness, but with excitement. Here, in the church, is the
window engraved by Lawrence Whistler to the memory
of Edward Thomas, poet, and Helen his wife who lived
near by. Snatches of the poems frostily etched there in
glass came into my mind as I walked along, particularly:

> *This is my grief. That land,*
> *My home, I have never seen;*
> *No traveller tells of it,*
> *However far he has been.*

It was something to think about as I headed towards
Wales, that land which Thomas loved so much and which
we who are drawn to it by temperament and ties of blood
see not merely as somewhere 'over the hills and far away'
but almost as Vaughan's visionary country, the country of
the soul, 'far beyond the stars'. No matter that Thomas was
not a theist like Vaughan. You have to be a doubter to be
a poet now.

It set me thinking, also, how many of our great poets
loved walking: Wordsworth, Coleridge, Hardy, Thomas –
to name only four – and how they were never less lonely
than when they walked alone. I should develop this theme,
I decided, as I struck into Lambourn, satisfied that I had
done the first seven miles of my journey in under two
hours.

It seemed I was too early to see any racehorses about.
Bockhampton Stables was to let – a sign of the times. I
passed the Lamb at Lambourn on my right, the Nippy
Chippy on my left and a series of small tokens of materi-

alism, palaces of refreshment for cars or their owners; then came my first string of racehorses and their jockeys, all silky and up-on-their-toes, all smiling and polite. This was a welcoming place, an impression confirmed by the inscription over the lych gate by the church COME UNTO ME ALL YE WEARY AND HEAVY LADEN AND I WILL GIVE YOU REST. I cast my burden on the Lord, and my haversack on the seat obligingly placed near by, and changed my socks in full public view. (There were children already on their way to school.) A blister was beginning to form on one foot. The first of a few?

Thinking of all the pilgrims who had passed this way – including Great Alfred, maybe – I stamped my trusty feet into my less than trusty boots and mounted like an eagle over the Downs. I had rehearsed all this in my mind at home. From Upper Lambourn via Hangman's Stone, Wellbottom Down, Kingston Warren Down and Uffington Down I should reach the Manger on hallowed White Horse Hill. It was all gallops and green corn. There was a total absence of sheep.

'That's a good horse,' I said to a jockey who looked like Pat Eddery, perched on top of a grey seventeen-hander, dappled and coolly leading a string downhill through a belt of trees to the stable-block below.

'I wish he could gallop,' he said and, smiling, pointed me into Kingston village and up the hill again, by the edge of a cornfield where a single skylark, urgently surviving – his tribe's last troubadour? – was buffeted by the same mad wind that snatched Pat's words and hurled them into the coombe: 'It's a long – old – way!'

NO HORSES it said at the top. But there were furlong markers on either side of the track and mounting stands of wind-swept corn. It was sunless and raining – as it was when I turned right on the Ridgeway and descended by Blowingstone Hill, by old barrows and lynchets, ridge

and furrow remains, arthritic thorns, an empty land, to
Kingston Lisle. I saw no Manger; no White Horse. . . .

Uffington was electrified and dull, Fernham crepuscular,
and gloomy Little Coxwell a hindrance, delaying access to
its Great namesake where I was attacked by a dog.

So rough was it in Great Coxwell tithe barn that
most of the National Trust's pamphlets (50p) were freely
distributed by the wind. The great door was wide open.
There was no one about. At the near-by manor house the
washing machine finished its programme with a cough, as
I heard through the open door which was adorned with a
Neighbourhood Watch notice. I went away, brooding on
the structure of that Great Barn, massively stanchioned in
stone, timbered and tiled, casting its shadow on seven centuries of history, visited out of a sense of duty by thousands
like me; and thinking also of the thousands more who, in
the past, visited it for a different reason – to pay tithes.
The strength of that stubborn old image of extortionism!
As swingeing in its power to strangle as a gibbet.

I went on, brooding, to Badbury where I got lost in the
woods; to Faringdon and, by main, safe road, to Lechlade
where the sun came out and I picnicked on a table tomb
in the sweetest churchyard I had seen that day. I examined
the church: its bossy roof, its spacious fifteenth-century
arches, its beeswaxed woodwork, its creamy stone and
stained glass casting that predominantly blue and amber
light I hope to see in heaven.

It gave me strength to walk to Fairford, where the
church, at barely five o'clock, was locked. The wind stung
my knees, tears sprang from my eyes, my nose ran. It was
fifteen miles to Chedworth. Oh yes, I walked free; but I
had never deluded myself: when the time came to tighten
the tension, take up the slack, I would resort, if I had to,
to hitching a lift.

I presented a sad and sodden sight to the motorists who

drove swiftly out of town. The butcher boy told me there was a bus to Ciren, sometime after six; it stopped by the Bull, which was on the other side of the road. It doesn't, I told him. I had seen the five o'clock go straight down the street; you would have had to have wings to catch it.

Highwayman-style, I compelled the six o'clock to stop and asked its driver why he didn't pull over to the Bull.

'I'm on my way home,' was his full-stop reply.

Empty except for me and one other passenger, the bus hurtled past the Ampneys, and, in that heart-stopping manner cornering buses have of appearing to drive into walls before missing them, wound round back streets, then dwindled to a halt by Cirencester's massive church. There my cousin picked me up and whisked me by car to Chedworth, a hot bath, supper and bed. I had been on the road for thirteen hours. I did not need to count sheep.

'And the evening and the morning were the first day.'

# On Malvern Hills
# a marvel befell me

Chedworth means Cedda's homestead. Lucky Cedda!

Ken and Elizabeth Minshull, my cousins who live in the cottage at the top of Ballinger's Hill, are artists: he in wood, metal and stone; she in wool, embroidery silks and – poor Cedda may not have known this word – *cuisine*. Expert in gardening too, they have, by restoration and innovation, made old Armstrong's Cottage live. They were, I thought as I lay in bed at six o'clock on Thursday the 22nd of March, in the process of restoring me.

I tried to shake a leg. It did not appear to belong to me. I listed to the window sill. And what did I see? Red berries on a holly tree!

I hauled my ten stone five pounds to the bathroom. I'm in good shape, I told myself, but avoided looking in the mirror.

Back in the bedroom, I heard a chaffinch in the garden, which further restored my spirits. Chaffinches are artists in survival; they chip away at their tune, perfecting it, as they do their technique for living in an innovative world. They are persistently, irrepressibly bright. Like those extraordinary holly berries. I must ask about them, I told myself. Meantime, however, I was having trouble with my feet. And my knees. I walked as if I were wearing armour. I could not unstraighten my legs. I took a turn round the garden to supple up. Back in the kitchen, a cup of tea acted like a drug. Elizabeth came down.

'It *is* late,' she said – meaning the holly tree. 'It has flowers on as well.' We agreed it must be sheltered between the house and the top of the hill. And it had been very mild, so the birds had left it alone.

We talked about the 'hose-in-hose', the double primroses she has in her garden, and the cockerels I heard crowing across the valley.

'Everything echoes round here,' she said, bouncing a boiled egg onto my plate. 'You should hear the silver band playing carols at Christmas. They go round the houses. We can hear them when they're playing on the other side.'

'Christmas comes twice to you!' I imagined sun bouncing off trees and sound bouncing off Ballinger's Hill.

'The Romans had their vineyards on the other side of the valley. We still have some of their snails – Roman snails, do you call them? Great fat things!'

'Ah, the Roman Villa,' I said, shaking up my classical foundations and trying to unstraighten my knee. 'You may still hear the tramp of the legions marching. . . .'

'There was another Roman villa at Listercombe Bottom – that's the valley parallel to this. We go there deer-spotting sometimes.'

'And woodpecker-spotting,' said Ken, who joined us just as it was time for me to leave.

'Chedworth is like Dunchideock,' I said mysteriously.

'What do you mean?' asked Ken.

'Well,' said I, remembering a holiday in Devon, 'there are certain places that are so enchanting when you first come upon them you pray they will never be changed.'

'Like Ludlow.'

'And Selkirk.'

'And Barley Cove.'

'I must get going,' I said. The church clock was striking eight. I struggled into the straps of my pack. They pointed me in the direction of the Seven Tuns pub and the Withington road. I waved goodbye to my cousinly friends and silently prayed that I would soon bounce back.

I was grateful for the solid background information gleaned over breakfast, especially as, nearly walking on air,

I was faced with a fairy-tale view, straight out of 'Home-Thoughts, from Abroad'. The sun, like a cockerel, crowed all over the valley. The wind had swept the sky clear. A pear tree in blossom stood adorned like a bride. A brook bounced out of the rock by the Seven Tuns. Schoolboys, already waiting for their bus, bounced their shoulderbags onto the road. It was a top-of-the-mornin'-to-ye, bonny, bouncy day!

Turning right at the top of the hill, I struck onto the Withington road. I would recognize the old airfield, I had been told. What I was unprepared for was the sudden loss of a view. Up on this high plateau, I could not see Chedworth at all. Flat and two-dimensional was the earth up here. A dead chaffinch lay crushed in the middle of the road, one wing waving, like a chequered butterfly. A friendly breeze was trying vainly to breathe life into its one free limb.

Beyond the airfield I came to a 1 in 8 hill, a vista of folded hills and Withington Estate. Cars screamed up and down. I wouldn't buy a used car from any of you, I screamed back. I hoped I was not doing permanent damage to my cartilages. It was a long – old – way.

After the drop, it was lovely to go uphill, then onto a nice flat road, a lane following a stream – still the Coln? – meandering between alders under a permanent blue sky and high cottonwool clouds, with a chaffinch for company who was happy to be alive.

I will only note here my regret that I could not stop in Withington, that Foxcote was but a tantalizing glimpse of what must be everybody's Ideal Home and that much of the land in between seemed sadly empty to me. Where, I wondered, were the sheep? A few Jacobs, of course. And horses? One. I slapped the old fellow on the rump to congratulate him. And oaks? There was a noticeable absence of them in this landscape. Very little walling. No decent hedges. Crude barbed-wire and sheep-net fencing. Pylons galore. Traveller's joy just awakening in the hedge-row – new, green life springing out of straggly, strawy, last year's humped-up waste. I tired of the roller-coaster glacial escarpment, set aside aeons ago and colonised by blackthorn, now in full tin-plate bloom. My chaffinch kept up his little chip-chip. Ahead was a ploughed field, sun striking it tawny – tawny as the walls of Jerusalem. This, in contrast to the field on my right with what looked like last year's corn growing up again. A skylark flew across my bows, sweetening the air with his wind-swept song. Fields were now flatter and more fertile, tilled for potatoes, I should say. A maple in flower on my right caught the sun – lime green. A second tawny field stretched out to the sun. Rooks built high in a beech. (No elms for them for many a day.) One or two unspectacular oaks. Many, many ash. Willow-lined course of a stream.

The stream told all. Hello little stream! I welcomed him.

Reader, you know how a field can be beautiful? Just like a woman displaying herself in the sun, that tawny field was beautiful! So too the stream. So too the satin-coated rooks. There was a time when farmers introduced rooks to their land if they were unlucky enough not to have any.

I discussed all this with my friends over luncheon at Charlton Kings.

Mary Paget, an elderly archivist, petite and nimble-minded as Miss Marple, is good on sources.

'Everywhere you go in Charlton,' she said, 'you cross water. Almost every house of the old village had its own well. As to trees, I can show you exactly where the ridge of limestone ends and the oaks and clay begin.'

'Of course, our rooks have lost their lovely elms,' added Joan, her stepdaughter and near contemporary companion.

Mary has edited the newly published *A History of Charlton Kings* for the local history society. She has teeth which testify to the quality of the minerals in the water round here. Her views seemed to me as well targeted and objective as her keen blue eyes, and a powerful corrective to mine which are cloudy and greeny-grey. She emphasized points by punching the knuckles of both hands into the small of her back. Joan is likewise firm, but large and brown-eyed. The legato movements of her hands are those of a skilled sculptor and woodcarver. She loves trees.

'Another distinctive feature of the Cotswolds are the cowslips,' she continued. 'You won't find many primroses on the scarp.'

Her voice and good articulation reminded me of Marghanita Laski's. As we walked in the garden she patted a smiling doronicum on the head as if it were one of her children in the playground of Bishop's Castle Grammar School where she used to teach. It is an established garden running almost wilfully wild with creepers and ramblers, all-pervading tobacco-coloured wallflowers, dark-centred narcissi, rolling aubretia, striding daffodils and bossy dandelions: a paradise for cats and birds.

Indoors, the table was precisely and elegantly laid for our meal: ham salad, and strawberries set in a jelly.

'That way they remain whole and don't go to mush,' Joan explained. Joan is good with her hands: an essential qualification in a teacher, whether you are carving a piece of wood or moulding a child's career. She told me that at Bishop's Castle one of the rules was that if a child was allowed in the town during the lunch hour he was required, on returning, to show the teacher on duty what he had bought.

'Miss, I've bought a bull,' said John, 'but I've left him in his pen.' (The market was held in the street.)

'And that boy turned out to be an even better farmer than his father.' She smiled a well-satisfied smile.

There were more smiles when Mary told of her early days as an archivist in Shrewsbury.

'I had lodgings in College Hill,' she said, 'next door to Mrs Wynne Corrie's – you know, where you used to have your music lessons.'

Memory conjured up the Georgian drawing-room, the Broadwood and the broadloom, the garden beyond the French window, spacious, scented with roses and, if not actually pulsing with music, somehow expectant of it because Purcell's Golden Sonata was open on a music stand and Mrs Corrie's violin was never far away.

'We overlooked the Coach and Horses pub and, of an evening in summer, the landlady would leave a pint of beer on the window-ledge outside for the bobby to down on his beat. Talking of beat – hadn't you better go?'

They whisked me to the Metro stop, to save me walking into the town. The bus had gone.

'There's another in half an hour.' They whisked me to the church, pointing out the alteration to the west doorway, dating originally from 1190.

It is amazing what incumbents have done and undone in their churches in the past: painting and decorating and illuminating – sometimes stopping just short of throwing out the stained glass when they should have been feeding their sheep.

Here, however, the stained glass was secure. (A rose window dating from 1824 is modelled, I was told, on the one at St Mary's in Cheltenham, which I was urged to go and see.) The crusader's alms chest, hewn from a solid tree trunk with an iron, claw-like clasp, is so heavy it would take, they said, several men to haul it away. So much was safe!

Mary and Joan were deep into plans for celebrating their church's eight hundredth anniversary: they talked of a flower festival in the summer and, in October, a concourse of former curates – 'Those that are still extant, that is.'

'A hwyl come full circle,' I quipped, making a bad Welsh pun.

I caught the Metro and waved goodbye, wondering what they made of my butterfly's effort to extract nectar from their garden, their table and that great efflorescence of many centuries of rooted faith, their church.

To Cheltenham I came, and Tonypandy Man.

On arrival in the city – all shoe shops, banks and building societies – I did as I was bidden and sought out St Mary's: no easy matter in modern, high-rise Cheltenham. It is set in a place apart. Above the concourse of buildings which testify to the city's rank and reputation as a centre for health and wealth, St Mary's spire still struggles into view. I thought of my favourite hometown church, St Mary's in Shrewsbury, which also has a spire and celebrated stained glass; it too was once the principal church of the borough and now finds itself passed by.

St Mary's in Cheltenham was wonderfully light and airy inside; and companionable.

'Welcome,' said a little man, smiling and rising from a pew.

Long before he had told me that the church was nine hundred years old, that it once belonged to the Abbey of Cirencester, that it passed with the formation of the new diocese of Gloucester by Henry VIII from the old

45

diocese of Worcester ('They jobbed around then, didn't they?') . . . that six hundred years ago there were only six hundred people in Cheltenham ('The size of a large village today') . . . that it was condemned as unsafe at the beginning of last century, when along came Captain Skillicorne whose life work was to restore it . . . long before this, I had christened my informant Tonypandy Man. His voice and manner were identical to those of the former Speaker of the House of Commons.

'You weren't born in Cheltenham,' I said.

'No, but I've lived here since 1938.' His candid, cornflower-coloured eyes dared me to state otherwise.

'You sound just like Viscount Tonypandy,' I said.

'That's where I came from,' he affirmed. That sorted out, we could now get on with Captain Skillicorne.

What a remarkable old boy he must have been. 'Filling in the old crypt which was causing the church to sink, you see . . . enlarging the building in the process, reglazing the windows . . . it's mostly modern glass, you see. . .'

'I wonder what happened to the old?'

'. . . ay, you do wonder, that's right, but it's very handsome, this one donated by the joint masonic lodges . . . and now [sotto voce] I'll show you the rose window, but unfortunately someone's come along and put an airgun pellet through it, see? That hole up there, bottom right, isn't it sad [a white pock-mark petalled like a suture, spoiling the window's stunning wholeness of design, grievous as a broken-stringed lute] . . . it does happen, the majority of people are very nice of course . . . and another thing, there's an old stone coffin here, been outside since the time the crypt was closed – smashed last summer with a sledgehammer, isn't that sad. . ?'

'Extraordinary. But who'd walk around here with a sledgehammer?'

'. . . well, it's done at night, you see, there's no one

living here now, it's a business centre, no houses. . .'

'No Neighbourhood Watch?'

'. . . that's right, that's exactly it . . . d'you like the honey-coloured stone?'

'Yes, and the handsome – is it wagon? – roof.'

'And the ten commandments which some king ordered to be put up, now who d'you think would read all that?'

'You'd need a ladder.'

'Pity the poor man who had to engrave all that . . . the altar screen is remarkable too, donated by H.H. Martin, founder of Gloster Aircraft Company, you know, the figures can be taken out for dusting . . . nice, isn't it. . ?'

'There's a lovely echo in the chancel, I bet the choir sounds good.'

'. . . we haven't a choir, we have two churches. . .'

'No boys, because of no one living round here?'

'. . . no, the trouble is to get a choirmaster, that's the problem . . . it was Canon Bell who panicked when the Cheltenham Ladies' College came, this church wouldn't be big enough so he had a new one built . . . then they had their own chapel after all that. . .'

I had my pocket recorder on, so when I studied Captain Skillicorne's memorial I rehearsed its eulogy, for his and my delight. 'Taught by Dr Wilson, justly called the good bishop of the Island ['. . . that's the Isle of Man . . .'] he, quitting the sea, after forty years' service, resided some years in Bristol and in 1738 came to live upon their estate in this town ['. . . that's he and his wife, she was a Quaker, he was a property developer in a big way . . .']. Mrs Skillicorne, a Quaker, was buried in the Quakers' graveyard, 1779, a virtuous woman, a good wife and tender mother.'

'The boy who shot the pellet,' I said, 'should have read that, it might have deterred him.'

'Perhaps he couldn't read. The majority are very nice,

but a small hard core . . . I don't know why they do such things. . .'

'Someone should get hold of them by the scruff of the neck, which is no longer done.'

'. . . Oh no, some do-gooder would say you should take pity on them, you know . . . they destroy things which we enjoy . . . I love looking at that window . . . all day . . . there's just a small volunteer group of us who look after the church, otherwise we'd have to shut it. It's a beautiful building, we love it, we relieve one another. . .'

'How nice that you do, for people like me to enjoy it. So – ' as I began retreating ' – I'll remember Captain Skillicorne. It was lovely to meet you.'

'Bless you, sir.'

Well-blessed, I emerged from St Mary's. Wisdom did not utter her voice in the streets, but I caught an echo of a favourite text above the noise of the concourse of people and buildings: 'Her ways are ways of pleasantness, and all her paths are peace.'

All the way to Tewkesbury I reflected on the past and present wealth of Cheltenham. How much of it was derived from water, how much from sheep? How much from property developers like Captain Skillicorne? I concluded it was far from being the Holy City, the New Jerusalem that I was looking for; nor, perhaps, is it the City of Light it may think it is; but it has a fair claim to be called the City of Gold.

There is no doubt, of course, that the prosperity of Cheltenham and this whole area is founded on water. The Chelt or Rungebourne rises in Dowdeswell; and it was on the steep, curved descent by Dowdeswell House

– where a sun-loving weasel played on the patio – that I first noticed the enormous height of the trees, a sure indication of a good water supply. But there were other, smaller tell-tale signs such as the handwritten notices by the roadside COTSWOLD MUSHROOMS FOR SALE (more mushrooms than sheep) and, nearer the reservoir, an official warning to motorists TOADS CROSSING ¾ MILE AHEAD.

Significantly, it was just before I had reached Charlton, near the road to Seven Springs, that water entered my consciousness, I might almost say entered my brain. There was that sudden efflorescence of seagulls. I thought they had found a field under plough. They had, of course, found the Severn-Trent Water Authority's Reclamation Strategy K6. THESE GROUNDS ARE PRIVATE IN THE INTEREST OF PROTECTING THE PUBLIC WATER SUPPLY a large notice proclaimed.

'Ah,' said I, 'to go public you have to go private!' The seagulls, heron, coot, dabchick and mallard leaving chevronned tail-wakes in the air, knew no such human subtleties.

Water! The power of it, the wealth of the men who master it and market it!

For the rest of the day, I carried a pint flask of the expansive Severn-Trent Water Authority's product with me in my knapsack as I walked on towards the Malvern Hills. It was good to see them, drowned only in sunshine, their foothills clouded with sheep.

Crossing the Severn bridge at Tewkesbury were a young couple with two small children. The man took one piggy-back, the woman wheeled the other in a pushchair. The man kept a close grip on his dog. He was blind. He could not see those hills, the mill, the boatyard by the weir.

A few yards further on, I was reliably informed by a man with two dogs that the river coming in at King John's Island is the Stratford Avon and that it does not actually join the Severn till it reaches the second mill, up by the abbey; a case of one river courting another for a few hundred yards then deciding to marry at the church. Its course was channelled, the man told me, in 1100. What powers of engineering the Normans displayed!

More Severn-Trent Water Authority treatment works did not spoil my evening of the gladsome mind, if tired feet. I crossed the river again, gaining the Ledbury road. A little man, thumb-stick in hand, on a path sign, did not tell me where it went – of course.

The fields were smaller, tussocky, rougher now: as they are in Shropshire; the little streams ran deeper, slower, murkier. The roadside verges sported clover and daisies, inviting me to walk on grass. I stopped at a gateway in sight of Bredon Hill, attended by milkmaids (ladysmock) pear blossom and my faithful Chaffy. I should have my tea, I thought. A gate is good to lean on; and all you need for a table is a gate post. It is certainly a stable place to rest a flask of water. Gates – Heaven itself is adorned by gates!

Now I was within sight of the Malvern Hills which are, and always have been, a kind of paradise to me. No matter how many times I see them, they fill me with happiness. It is like catching anew the sight and smell of the sea; for, like the sea, the Malvern Hills are bedded deep in the consciousness of all true Englishmen.

My friend Audrey, to whose house in Colwall I was heading, exchanged the flat-race scene of Newbury for these delectable obstacles about ten years ago. I had roved over them many times before, having first heard of them when I was a boy at Little Ness. Older boys with drop-handlebarred bicycles returned one Sunday to tell of these hills as it were of a Promised Land: a soft land, undulating, not jagged and harsh like some of our mean Shropshire hills. They spoke of spas and holy wells and spring water gushing out of the hillside with which they splashed their faces, then filled cupped hands to drink. They told of a flat watery plain to the east, of castles and wooded old hunting grounds, and the wild hills of Wales to the west. They told of hop fields, oasts, orchards and fruits in abundance, as if it were the Garden of Eden. Perhaps it was because it was Sunday that these biblical images formed in my mind.

Later, it seemed even more like the Holy Land when I discovered that there were abbeys and priories and cathedrals all near by. They had such lovely soft-sounding names: Malvern, Worcester, Gloucester, Tewkesbury. . . . It was the beginning of the South Country: continue, head down, on a drop-handlebarred bike, and you might reach Bristol and the sea!

Those older boys told me how they had ridden along the crest of the Malverns in top gear, almost all the way. And when I walked it later my feet sprang off the sheep-cropped turf. Edward Thomas had walked here with Robert Frost who rented a house near Ledbury, Masefield's town, too. Langland trained as a priest at Malvern Priory. Audrey had told me how she drew water freely from the spring – water that was bottled and supplied to royalty. By appointment, I was going there now. Mentally, momentarily, I felt like a king.

My stomach was restored, but I had a king-sized ache in my knees. Someone, it seemed, had rapped them with an iron bar. Soreness had set into my feet. Good Deeds said 'Attend to it.' Obstinacy: 'What with?' I knew I was on a pilgrimage compounded of pleasure and pain; that every time I laughed I would wince – and every time I winced I'd laugh. I walked with the Lord.

Halfway up a high hill was a lady by a stationary car. She directed her gaze at me. She returned to the car and got in. She appeared to be reversing. She was. She got out.

'Oh,' she exclaimed, 'I was hoping you were somebody else!' – and she drove off. And there was I, Christian with his burden, the Little Mermaid walking on knives. I had been close enough to her estate car to see a notice in the rear window. She was concerned with Ledbury point-to-point. The grass on which I was trying to walk had been rendered rough by horses' hooves. I drew my own conclusions.

Minutes later, a man in a cattle wagon with a collie in the cab picked me up.

'Wonderful,' I gasped, my tongue and the collie's lolling in sympathetic harmony.

'I've been in the same situation myself,' said the driver, who was going to Ledbury. Justice done, he set me down on the road to Colwall, with instructions on how to proceed. I hobbled up another hill. To my right was a stream in a deep valley gorge, surprisingly almost empty at this time of year. Coming out of the hills, you would expect to find it full. Cherry blossom, and the new green leaf of nut and hawthorn sprang to life – and something that defeated me: was it hornbeam with its tufted, flake-like bracts? At last I spotted a good-sized oak, patting his lichen-crusted bole, like Falstaff his belly, in the evening sun.

At the end of the Malverns I was to look for a dilapidated garage, the road to British Camp (not to be taken) and Colwall, round the back. I was assured it was not too far.

Moving on, I was enchanted by the numbers of old pear trees which stood around, alone or in twos and threes in old orchards, by farms, long, long neglected. I don't think farmers make perry now.

Steep and rugged was my pathway. Suddenly I beheld a burning bush. A poplar, was it? Lit by the setting sun, it looked like the great west window of an abbey – a Jesse window, perhaps. It might have been – was I deceived? – the Tree of Heaven! It stood about a hundred yards to the right of a little church: All Saints, Hollybush.

Was this where I was told to turn, I tried to recollect. Or just a little further on? This was an off-centre community. The houses, further up the hill, taking shelter from the trees. The stand-offish church was left to the common and the sheep. There was a stunning crop of gorse.

I digested the Malvern Hills by-laws (act of 1924) and, discovering myself to be an unauthorized person, pressed on. Coming now to the settlement itself, I reasoned that this was one of those villages which became isolated by the Plague. A bungalow called Bredon View had an uninterrupted outlook on that hill, spanning a settlement of farms, some untidiness in the middle distance, but mostly open fields and what looked like common land. It seemed to be all down to grass. There were a few tumbledown barns – a sight for unsore eyes. But where were the people? My team was not still ploughing. . . .

Up among the houses, however, in the shelter of hillside trees, I heard an eerie creak. A peacock, perhaps? A magnolia shone with all lamps lit. In the same cottage garden on the hill, a barred-rock cockerel – his tail a quiverful of sunbeams – coaxed his dozen wives into a pen for the night. There was birdsong, sheepsong, a cock pheasant sounding off in the wood. This, I could truly say, was the Valley of Delight.

I found a kiosk by a little farm and phoned my friend. 'Stay where you are!' She would come and pick me up. In a halo of birdsong and pear blossom – and, it has to be said, content – I sat on a low wall by forsythia and flowering currant and watched – it's true! – a shepherdess feeding her ewes and lambs. She called them, they hurtled down the hill at sight of her and the sound of the sheep nuts rattling into their troughs. 'Come on, come on!' she called – as if they needed to be told! I conducted a vain conversation with her, against the happy hubbub of rollicking lambs and anxious ewes and the Scottish collie playing the bagpipes at the gate. 'I've only been doing it for two years. . .' Shepherdess screamed '. . . I haven't made any money yet!'

Why bother about money? I wanted to ask.

'Stay there. . . I'll come and talk. . . .' But my friend rolled up in her car and whisked me, defeated, to Colwall, to a hot bath, supper and bed. Ah, welcome defeat!

# I Meet a Man who has Sized Up Life

Restored by surgical spirit to walking order, I set off from Colwall next morning at seven to find the Mathon road. (Mathon rhymes with Nathan.) Following my friend's instructions, I turned left out of Oak Drive, then took the second turn on my right. I passed a fine house built by some prosperous Welshman, no doubt, and christened Llanwriarth. I rolled it round my tongue – the name, that is -- and savoured it. The quality of housing in these parts was high. It matched the quality of the views. Are there, I wondered, any hills in the world more classically composed than the Malverns? Mozart might have had a hand in the laying out of their parts: their harmonious grouping, perfect in form and line. Here fields had oaks and sheep aplenty; they ranged beyond where ploughs could operate. The splash-faced sheep (already looking Welsh: Kerry Hill or Beulah, perhaps) matched the handsome half-timbered houses, fronted by magnolias and thronged with blackbirds chanting their aubades. No one – not even the most spirited lamb – was abroad at this early hour. They were all couched, close to one another, belly to belly and back to back, reliving the dreams of the night.

This, to my mind, is the authentic picture of sheep: possessing the land, as they have since Abraham's time. You cannot imagine these fields without their close-quartering sheep; and their oaks, dotted about.

A mile further on, I passed four Suffolk rams round a cratch filled with hay, building themselves up, in a paddock on my left; and, on my right, more free-range ewes that, at some signal from the matriarch, had decided to go early to work, leaving their lambs lying down.

A schoolboy, rucksack on his back, the cup of his flask peeping out, cycled by. He had a harder day ahead than I!

A black and white farmhouse – not associating itself with the three tractors, a caravan, a barn and what looked like a covered wagon opposite – had beams all beautifully pegged. I failed to note the name. Ahead were polythene arcs and domes, ash trees, a pick-up, but no one about. I took it to be a nursery. I wandered in.

'Hello,' I said to a young man stooping over baby conifers. 'Can you tell me the name of the black and white house?'

'The Hacketts,' he said.

'It's properly timber-pegged, authentic, very fine. Is it the farmhouse?'

'It belongs to an agricultural contractor,' he smiled. 'Actually, it's two knocked into one.'

'You're not the nurseryman?'

'No, I'm just working here. For experience. Hope to have my own nursery in two years' time.'

'Good for you!' He didn't seem to think I was odd, expecting to get to Stockton today.

'Any blisters?'

Seeing his open smiling face, I had to admit I had.

'Nice to meet somebody!' I said.

'Have fun!'


I came to Tower House Farm where a collie was rounding up geese. I first spotted them at the back of a barn, the collie laughing and salivating, head-down, at its outraged captives with their backs to the wall and their gawky heads up. It teased them along a causeway leading to the farmyard and the house. I left my grandstand view by the hedge and tiptoed down the drive, meaning to ask about the very early plum blossom I kept seeing round here. Farmers do not answer front-door visitors, so I padded like the preoccupied dog round the back.

'Your dog,' I said to the man who opened his kitchen window to have words with me, 'is rounding up the geese.'

'Oh, she's full o' work,' he sang, crisp bacon rind spilling from his mouth. 'Lovely dog – all her pups have done well.'

We chewed times over, old and new. 'Yes, yes, the Kerries still do well – crossed now, of course. . . . The blossom's early, isn't it? Whatyamacallit – stuff they used to make gin with. . . . Lovely orchards up where you're going, Suckley and Stockton way. . . . Oh, I know Bill – used to go with him to Tenbury market. Remember me to him. Those were the days!' (Bill is the farmer at Stockton who had told me I should be welcome to call anytime.)

Interlarded, so to speak, was more information about the Hacketts.

'Belongs to John Bevan . . . does my contracting. Too many contractors about these days, but John's a decent fella, no messing. . . . Yes, yes. Well, it's nice to have met you . . . I think you're a very nice fella to talk to . . . yes, indeed.' He closed the window. The dog was still holding the geese.


I made my way past genuine half-timbered houses – mostly on my left, I noticed – and stone houses, painted, aping them on my right, the less sunny side.

There was every kind of proper sheep here: Suffolk and speckle-faced, either Kerry or Beulah – and Mules of course. Every farm had its orchard of old-time apples and pears, the latter now a show. I was still perplexed by plantations of early-flowering plum – surely not sloe. Black and white collies came out to inspect me with light, foxy eyes. This was all good farming country, small-scale, still neighbourly, with little settlements of houses round farms

– and huge manure heaps, good to see and smell at this time of day. I was nearing the end of the Malvern range, accompanied, as I had been all the way, by creaking trees and chaffinches. I know what I'm doing, I told myself: I'm repairing the omissions of my youth. I should have come here before.

I just could not make that blossom out. Damson? Perhaps, but for some reason I thought not. The hills were lovely. And the oaks. Young oak leaves in spring – baby-fisted, catching the light and holding on to it like coins of gold. Strong white houses, with whitening orchards round about. White-faced houses, that is. Red-brick barns (they didn't want the house to look like the barn so they painted it). One barn blown to smithereens by last month's gales. And, after that, some smart parkland; distinguishable by the height of the trees: cedar, chestnut, whitebeam – 'aery abeles' – douglas fir. This was what I came to see!

GOD HAS ALREADY PITCHED HIS TENT IN THE 21ST CENTURY said a notice outside Mathon church. The old yew pitched his some centuries before.

'Well done, you lads!' I said to two young men repairing the road in front of the church. 'More good road for me to walk on.'

'That's it.'

QUALITY HOMES FOR THE DISCERNING BUYER ... Oh dear!

I stopped to ease my blisters. Waved down a roadman's lorry. It's the two lads.

'It's a long old way up to Suckley!' (I didn't tell them I was going to Llanrhaeadr.) 'Where are you going after Suckley?'

'Stockton on Teme.'

'That's where my mate comes from,' said the boy

at the wheel.

'Does he know Bill Sinnett?'

'I know Bill. You goin' to see 'im? 'e'll get the Scotch out.'

They drove on. They all thought it was a long – old – way. I laughed – not so much at my folly as at their doubting my experience.


I came to Cradley next, than which I doubt Polperro has more tiny houses clinging to its hill. The great square church had room for residents and visitors as well, but I passed on. It was a long – old – way.

Worcestershire, warm and bosomy, unfolded ahead. Hopyards strode, their strings and poles symmetrically set out. Bonsai'd apples lined the roadside fields. Landscape plotted and pieced . . . reek of ammonia – chlorine perhaps? A notice on a gate said PVW KEEP OUT. No lamb bleat from hilly bourn. I met no man to ask about those plums. I felt unwanted here.

A man appeared – the last on earth! He was huddled over his lunch by a barn. KEEP OUT said the notice on the gate. The man was furtive, fumbly, toothless and old – a little end-game man. He had thistledown hair, necromantic eyes, an outsize muffler, fingers like Jerusalem artichokes and a Scots accent.

'It's a decease!' he said, with frightening finality.

'Oh! And what are these early plums?' I asked, more mindful of the living than the dead.

'Plumps? I dinna ken – sumps redd, sumps bloo!' He stuffed another piece of bread into his mouth to shut me up.

I examined the hop-poles whose strings appeared to be looped over transverse wires at the top: up two, down one – knit two, purl one. . . There was a lot of money tied up there.

I came to a farm. I wandered in.

'What's PVW?' I asked a young man in a cattle shed.

'It's the wilt on the hops.'

'I shan't be drinking any beer for a while. You just keep beef cattle?'

'Only beef.'

He was a nice lad: monosyllabic as intensive agriculture requires.

I next met a man walking, carrying an elder tree on his back.

'I'm a dedicated wine-maker,' he said. Now, deep in my subconscious lurked the idea that it is unlucky to traffic in elder trees.

'Are you going to plant it?'

'No, burn it. It fell in the gale and a friend asked me to clear it out. It's a white elder. Rare.'

'You mean the berries are white?'

'The berries is white.' He struggled on with his burthen. A dedicated wine-maker – a rare thing to meet in the middle of the day.

I passed by a lodge and a bridge over the Teme where I had my lunch. Always by water I observed those tufted flake-like seeds. Strange, I thought, how you can live to nearly three score years and ten and be defeated by the identity of such a common thing.

I pondered on, past a grand house on a hill. Its mellow sandstone gables and mullions matched the Charolais and Simmental bulls at peace in a field on the opposite side of the road. Not many people can afford to keep bulls.

ANDREW GRANT SITE SALE ROOM said a notice next to a family of oasts as I entered Suckley: were these the Tele-hamlets I had read about in the *Daily Telegraph*? A great three-storey house, cheese-coloured, with a fine shell porch surmounted by a coat-of-arms, stared blindly onto the road, uncertain of its future, reflecting on its past. Other houses had an odd assortment of names: one called 'Knightsbridge' was offering Levington Compost at £5.10 a bag.

Assorted sheep reared after plum leaves: blackface, blue-face, speckled and white. They pivoted on their hindquarters like goats. They reaped the harvest of the storm.

Tiring of Suckley – it's a long old way – my heart leaped up when I beheld real Hereford cattle, the first I'd seen; and a real Hereford house, red brick, barge-boarded, gabled and sash-windowed – all that a Hereford house should be. It was probably the herdsman's house. The farmhouse proper stood back in its park. I thought it had a mansard roof. It was elegantly set about with trees, a great number of which were of a kind not seen much nowadays, the one so wisely planted by old furniture-loving farmers: the walnut.

Sheep and cows 'peopled' the park. At the entrance to the long sweeping drive tottery day-old lambs – twins – exulted in the wind, shaking their tails and guzzling milk from their dams. Here, facing two towering horse-chestnut trees, my knees protesting, I leant my back against a good-sized oak.

The Lord of the Manor drove in with his BMW and Lord-of-the-Manor look. I would not have swapped my Mars Bar for his dinner – but he clearly took me for a tramp.

It was nearly dark when I arrived at 92 Worcester Road, Stockton-on-Teme. A spade stood ready to hand by the door.

'I'll dig!' I said to the man who answered my knock.

'Are you Mr Sinnett?'

I had heard of Bill, and he of me, but this was our first meeting. He is a legend among farmers and stockbreeders.

'I am – and you're Peter Davies. Come in, you look as if you could do with a drink.'

Taking off his cap, for he had only just finished in the garden, Bill led me into the house.

'Mary!' No reply. He showed me to a comfortable armchair. 'My wife must have popped out to look in on her aunt.' He moved about in distant regions of the house. 'I'll get you a cup of tea. How far've you come today? . . . Colwall? That's further than some people walk in a year. You'd better stay the night . . . we've got plenty of room. You can have a bath, there's plenty of hot water. I bet you're stiff. . . .'

'All I want is to take my boots off.'

'Go on, do. . . Sugar? Here, put these slippers on.'

The smile that accompanied these offerings was that of the father to his prodigal son. I started to tell him where I'd been. Pershore's Juice, a famous Hereford bull, whose portrait hung on the wall, looked steadfastly at me. And so did Bill.

A short, clean and shiny man, upright in khaki tweed and cavalry-twill, his dark, sleek hair belies his years. He is well past three score years and ten, and has now given over the farm – Stockton Court – to his sons. He and his wife moved into the workmen's cottages, previously semi-detached, now knocked into one.

It took him no time at all to tell me about this. He is a rapid communicator, Bill, with a full diapason of views and voice to match; a good host, wide-ranging in his interests, with that ability to offer you, the visitor, the floor that is the gift of the fulfilled man. He has the keen eye and intelligent head of a greyhound, though he does not much resemble a greyhound in other respects, being rather too round; but he has rolled successfully through eighty years and looks as if he will roll a long while yet.

He saw me looking at the bull.

'You won't see many like him today.'

I told him about the Herefords I had seen on my way.

'Walker's,' he affirms. 'One of the last of the pedigree herds. Round here, that is. And then you came through Whitbourne?'

'Then Clifton. Then I lost my way.'

'Through Great Witley?'

'I don't know. I thought I could drop down over the fields to Stockton. The lad in the butcher's shop said the path went from somewhere by the church. First I couldn't find it at all. Then I came to some look-out huts. I thought they might be for the use of the shepherds – seeing so many sheep around.' The smile broadened on Bill's face. 'Then loudspeakers sprouted from poles, cables looped, and benches sprang up on the hill.'

'You came down the hill climb!'

'It tested my knees!'

'Then Stanford Bridge? It's a long old way, even from there. He came down Shelsley hill climb, Mary. Hey, we're missing "Surprise, Surprise!"'

Mary came in, still in her coat. She is small, quiet and evidently capable. She has pretty white hair and blue, smiling eyes which invite the stranger to feel at ease in her company, better than words.

'Put it on,' was all she said and turned to do some other task.

'We love Cilla, don't we, Mary?'

'There's not much left of her.'

'This lad here's just walked from Colwall. He'd better stay the night.'

'I'll put the blanket on. We'll just see the end of

the programme, then we'll have supper.'

Cilla puts all to rights. Noothing is too much trooble. 'Isn't that loovlee?'

We repaired to the kitchen. The table was mysteriously already set for three.

Nothing is too much trouble for Mary and Bill. Goodness shines out of their eyes.

'I'll show you round the farm in the morning,' said Bill. 'You'd better not lock the door in case you can't get out of the bath.'

'I've put you some Lloyd's cream to rub on your knees.' Mary has been a nurse. 'It's a famous old remedy.'

'Loovlee,' I said, thinking of Cilla Black waving her television wand and reuniting friends and families sundered for years. Bill and Mary, who had never set eyes on me before, resolved all my problems in one evening: PVW (Progressive vertical wilt); the early-flowering plum (damsons, of course); the tufted flake-like seeds (hornbeam); and my knees (Lloyd's cream).


'I am fearfully and wonderfully made,' I exclaimed as I examined myself in the bathroom next morning. I still walked like someone newly released from Stoke Mandeville. I had three black toenails and blisters on both feet, but they were not weeping – yet. The Lloyd's cream had worked wonders – not to mention the hot bath and warm bed, into either of which you could have sunk Pershore's Juice. Looking out of the bedroom window, which gave a view of the garden, the church and Stockton Court, and everywhere eyefuls and earfuls of lambs, I hoped Bill did not plan to take up my last evening's offer to dig.

The house, I realized as I went downstairs, was more spacious than I had thought last night.

'I couldn't live in a poky place,' said Bill. 'It took a bit of getting used to, mind, moving from the Court.'

'Well, we've got such big furniture, you see,' Mary added.

'We manage,' said Bill. 'How's the legs? You walk like a man on sawn-off stilts.'

We sat down to a farmhouse breakfast, Bill counting out his pills on his plate, as much in charge of this part of his destiny as he is of the rest.

'I'll show you the sheep, then we'll go to Clifton for the weekend joint; then John and David might have finished what they're doing and you can have a talk with them.'

Bill was happy and relaxed, this fine Saturday morning in spring, and impressed me by both his modesty and his pride.

'You only need a little fire to warm yourself – a big one can burn you,' is one of his favourite sayings. 'It's the truth that hurts' is another. He is good on the folly of borrowed money. 'And you cannot spend what you have not earned. Farming, like every other industry, to be successful, has to have three things. . .' (I waited while the formula was properly chewed) '. . . Capital, Management and Labour.' He is excellent on bureaucratic politicians: 'They canna see a 'ole in a ladder!' Cobbett would have loved Bill's company.

Later that morning we went by Vauxhall Cavalier to see the rams. Tups, Bill calls them: seven special Suffolks in a patch apart.

'Seven judges would each pick a different one as the best,' he assured me, after putting me to the test. He pointed out one that cost several thousands of pounds. 'But he may not be the best. I go by their ears.' He conjured up another *bon mot*: 'It's the foot of a horse, the muzzle of a beast, and the ear of a sheep that counts.'

To Bill all cattle are beasts. I trembled to think what value he put on me.

Is there nothing he has not sized up? I asked myself.

And, quick as I could blink, I was in Clifton upon Teme, in the presence of the butcher boy who put me on my way to Stockton yesterday. Bill was given a joint the size of which I had not seen since the war. Its provenance was no doubt guaranteed. After another social call, we drove back to the farm. To David and John.

I was staggered by John. I think he said he had delivered fifty lambs already that morning. He and David were so busy, I did not ask either to say anything twice. After a brief visit to the house, we were on our way down to the lambing sheds. They had a thousand Mules lambing, those two lads.

'As quick as you do one, there's another on the go!' As soon as possible, the lambs (mostly twins) and their mothers had to be loaded onto the big lorry and despatched to pastures far afield. In all this sweaty activity I stood around, looking, as my father used to say, like a useless article.

David and John picked up lambs in twos, one in each hand, and dropped them on the lorry floor.

'They're tough – they have to be.'

I cottoned onto the swift manipulation of the retaining gates and made sure only the right ewes went forward to join their bewildered and clamouring offspring. The lorry soon filled up. We jumped aboard and reversed the process at a roadside field a mile or so away.

'It's an eighteen-hour day,' said John; but he still had time to show me his special flock of thirty Suffolks and their lambs before I left. Some had been topped off (their backs shorn, flat as table tops) in preparation for showing. One lamb, born in January, was already worth several thousands of pounds.

'Silly money,' said John. 'Look at the width of his head!' His weight (the lamb's) was forty kilos. 'There's a quarter of a million pounds' worth of lambs in this field,' he said, waving one hand abroad and putting the other to his head. Talking money, it seemed, was like swearing: a dash stood for unmentionable thousands of pounds. The bankers were the new masters in the farm business, he said. The pressure to succeed is ultra-intense. 'And a ram only has to have too narrow a head or not enough thigh-muscle. . . .'

'Or too small ears?' I smiled – succeeding, I hoped, in my apprenticeship. I was reminded of the grey horse I'd been impressed by near Lambourn – a picture of dappled elegance: the horse that couldn't gallop.

John delivered me back to his dad.

Back in the house, Mary was preparing lunch. 'You won't go without something to eat?' she said. 'I'd like to give you something.' So I sat down to a bowl of raspberries and cream.

'I'll see you on your way,' said Bill, who really seemed to think I might have been a worthwhile apprentice, if I had persevered. *En route* to Clows Top, I rehearsed some of his teaching, and tried to encompass his philosophy.

'In a nutshell,' he said, 'it's "do unto others as you would they should do unto you." ' There, at a triangular road junction I said goodbye to Bill; a man, it seems to me, who has sized up life.

# A Hill called Difficulty

Cleobury Mortimer. One o'clock. Temptations lined the hilly street. Lunch at a café, beer at a pub, a Tango at the paper shop? Refreshment was on offer everywhere. I chose the church. It did not say: 'He that drinketh of the water that I shall give shall never thirst'; but there was a surprise here that took my breath and worldly appetite away: the East window.

Window: eye of the wind. What an exciting word that is; and how much more so if we think of wind as spirit.

In the East men do not set so much store by windows as we do in the West. If Christ had been an Englishman he might have said, 'Behold, I stand at the window and lift you up' rather than 'Behold, I stand at the door and knock,' for Christ has surely come to more people through windows than through our stout – and often locked – church doors.

Think of the elevation of spirit experienced on a visit to such early Christian foundations as Fountains Abbey where there are no doors and those windows that are left are rather enhanced than 'ruined' because they have no glass. Think of Haughmond Abbey in Shropshire where the West window, that great arch of mediaeval masonry, opens like an eye on the whole Shropshire Plain. Or think of Tintern, the apotheosis of the pointed arch which, sunk in a wooded valley, seems not to watch but to sleep, disregarding the world outside its walls.

But to return to Cleobury Mortimer. A board in the church porch tells you that William Langland 'according to a well-authenticated tradition' was born in the town here and educated at the nearby Augustine Monastery of Woodhouse and later at Great Malvern Priory. . . . Langland, whose neglected classic of the fourteenth century, *Piers Plowman*, goes with me on all my travels for courage and good company.

Like Dante's *Divine Comedy* and Milton's *Paradise Lost*, *Piers Plowman* deals with the largest of themes: the meaning of man's life on earth. But it is far earthier than either of those rather extra-terrestrial dreams – though still visionary, and as unpredictable as any dream. Langland goes banging on like a grim blacksmith, turning his ideas like pieces of iron, reheating them in the furnace of his imagination, returning to his desk (iron-hard as an anvil) to hammer out more words, testing them all the time with his stern eye for toughness and truth. He plunges all his pieces in turn into a tank of cold water, hissing like demons, for Pride in their creation might be accounted a sin, and Excitement be found damnable like any other heat of the blood. They lie higgledy-piggledy about the floor of his forge; you can pick them up in any order and test them one by one, as he did, for truth. But you need a good eye – and some hard-won experience.

Inscribed on the board in the church porch, is a quotation from Langland's poem – rather chastening, I thought:

> *Holy Church am I, quoth she,*
> *Thou oughtest to know*
> *'Twas I received thee first*
> *And thou the Faith did'st teach.*
> *To me they brought your sureties*
> *My bidding to fulfil*
> *That thou would'st love me loyally*
> *Thy whole life through.*

No half measures there! There may be some doubt about William Langland's birthplace, but none at all about his message. As you open the door of this lofty parish church of St Mary the Virgin you feel you are heading for something big. And there it is – mainly thirteenth and fourteenth century but heavily restored and embracing many architectural styles – all revelatory and light.

It is no small pleasure to enter a church that is light. This, like the one at Shelsley Walsh, is also warm.

I carried the memory of that gem at Shelsley Walsh like an amulet: a pocket-sized touchstone by which to measure the awfulness of other restorations of the time. It is perhaps easier to be small and well-preserved. This beautiful church at Cleobury Mortimer manages to go one better and be big.

This, I thought, is a sympathetic church. The pillars leaned outwards like my legs, showing the strain that corporeal development of one kind or another over the years had placed on them. In some contrary, homeopathetic way it uplifted me.

I was drawn, of course, to that East window. I felt I had to give it due attention, to work at it – even to the point of drawing it out on a scrap of paper, to help me retain some of those visionary images.

The work of one Harry John Burrow, about 1872, it is heavily influenced by the pre-Raphaelite movement in art. There are three soaring panels. At the base is the dedication: IN MEMORY OF WILLIAM LANGLAND, POET, WHO SANG JESUS CHRIST IN THE VISION OF PIERS PLOWMAN. At the foot of the centre panel Piers lies asleep and dreaming, his shepherd's crook resting on the ground by one hand, his head supported by the other, and the Malvern Hills jutting rather too jaggedly behind. Robed rather monkishly in a brown overall with hood, he looks like Lob, earth-spirit of Old England, whose 'home was where he was free'. He is shaped like a recumbent ox. There are lily pads on a pond in the foreground, as untroubled as the expression on the dreamer's face. There is at first no suggestion of the Harrowing of Hell.

71

Above the sleeping Piers are the words DO BEST; then Mary of Magdala with foxy-coloured Burne-Jones hair kneeling at the feet of Jesus; then the Ascension with attendant disciples; then Christ in Majesty.

In the left-hand panel Truth stands on the battlements of a stylised castle, such as you might see in Tennyson's *Idylls of the King*, holding up a mirror in her right hand; then there are the words DO WELL; then a representation of Christ's first miracle, wine jars to the fore; then the Roman centurion Jairus and his daughter; and, at the top, a knight kneeling with his lady and a courtly squire. DO WELL appears to have rather more well-to-do aspirants than the panel on the right, devoted to DO BET (the 'TER' is left out). Here we see Falsehood standing among thistles and flowers (no heavenly battlements) with a skull in his hand; then the Last Supper with evident suspicion falling on the red-headed Judas; then the crucifixion itself; and, most significantly perhaps, another lord and his lady kneeling – not so finely dressed as their counterparts on the left – a coiffed attendant, yes, but twined foliage and temptation in the form of a red apple suspended overhead.

While I was standing there looking at the East window, marvelling at all this pre-Raphaelite composure (and class distinction) I thought of Edward Thomas – the only other poet I know who has a church window dedicated to him with his words inscribed to such telling and simple effect. Dear, sweet, doubting Thomas! He shared with Langland so many things: a deep attachment to these half-Welsh hills; joy in the company of birds, trees and Nature generally; a mistrust of book-learning, preferring the direct evidence of his senses; poverty; an uncompromising regard for truth; humour; gloom; and that prescient spirituality – immanence, I believe is the word for it – which Wordsworth also had in abundance, which gives the seer no easy view of heaven, or even of this imperfect world, but a shatter-

72

ingly clear vision of the awfulness of Hell.

I left the town – the field full of folk – and took to the common, the field full of sheep. There were some people and cars here, too, but mostly I had the world to myself. A world of silver birch, short grass, bright gorse and ancient common rights. Like making water on the ground – and surprising only a blue-rinse ewe.

As I made my way from one Cleo or Clee to the next (Cleobury was now behind me and Clee Hill and Cleeton St Mary ahead) I puzzled over the origin and meaning of Cleo and Clee. Surely they meant clay. But the church guidebook said no, the hills were of stone. '*Kle* which is Old Norse for a stone used as a weight in a loom, seems more appropriate.'

Cars whizzed past on bright Macadam roads towards Clee Hill. My knees were in no mood to tackle that. I stuck to common trails furnished with cattle grids and scuffed, pan-scrubber turf. I sniffed the liberating steel-bright air. Freedom enlarged my lungs. My expectation levels rose. The natives were friendly, the visitors few. The odd car stopped and the ever-watchful in-lamb ewes gathered round like little village housewives to see what the local delivery van had brought.

Hopton Wafers, Silvington, Farlow. . . . They were not on my bee-line map, villages with pretty names, small-holdings, left-over implements, and temporary sheet-iron sheds. Lane End? It did not seem to have an end. I asked a young man toiling in his garden if I was right for Cleeton St Mary.

'Well, it's a long way round,' he said, dropping his spade, raising his cap, wiping his brow, and pointing in the direction of storm-troubled, cloud-capped Wenlock

Edge. 'I should go back to Silvington, myself.'

He knows, I thought. He was born at Farlow. I was pleased to have spoken to such a promising lad, proud of his roots and, after restoring his cottage, making such a good job of his garden. I wished him luck. He wished me the same.


It was a long old way through Silvington again. The wind had intensified, the temperature dropped to zero, or thereabouts, I should think. Light rain turned to splintering sleet.

I was going downhill. Now roadside streams caught flying flakes of snow. It was growing dark. I passed a farm where sheep were safe within the fold, sorting through their silage heaps, speckle-faced and unalarmed. I, speckle-faced with snow, grew ever more alarmed. Cleeton St Mary 4, a signpost said. Another hand pointed to Bouldon. Cleeton St Mary I chose, thinking a place with a name like that must have a bed.

It had a Hill of Difficulty. It had *son et lumière*. Snow had settled on Titterstone Clee. The sun was playing on it. Thunder clouds, the colours of iron drawn out of a furnace, red and indigo, rolled overhead. Domes, dishes and aerials looked like the gods' maths workshop on top of the hill. The sun toyed fitfully with them, turning their white to gold.

Whenever sun came out, campion and stitchwort smiled. Then the sun went in – this time for the night. I was nearly run over by a car. It splashed through the ford. A notice nailed to a tree said PLEASE DRIVE SLOWLY. Lambs in a field close to a house looked just like kittens. Up popped the steeple of a church. Down sank the running brook, under a bridge. Still waters, green pastures. . . . You can't stay here, I told my faltering feet.

I could not shake off that hill with its Wagnerian overtones, its melodramatic sky effects and those damned instruments, the radar aerials with their extraterrestrial look.

A lady in the churchyard dressing a grave did not know who did B & B.

'Ask that lady up there,' she said. The lady a little way along the road, seeing me wave, disappeared into the house. Church Cottage, it was called.

The clouds were very angry now – the colour of the bruises on my feet. The hills stood dressed with snow, and lit by ungodly light. A curlew bubbled over the plain. A sign that my trials were over, perhaps.

A perfectly normal young couple in a car stopped and asked me if I would like a lift. They took me about a mile and directed me to a bed and breakfast place on the main road. I thanked them, thinking my troubles were over at last.

'No, I haven't a vacancy,' said a lady, who had first looked out and seen me coming. Her husband was away. 'Try over the road.'

Over the road, a young man came to the door, leaned on the jamb and called into consultation another young man.

'We used to,' the consultant declared. 'Try up the road. They don't have a sign out, but they take people in.'

I tried up the road. It seemed like a farm. I worked my way by a dark passage past barking sheep-dogs to an unlit back door.

'Good boy, good boy. . . .' A yard of pump water, a fellow in a cap, jerkin and jeans, answered the door.

'Do you do bed and breakfast?' I asked.

'I'll have to see,' he said, retreating to Götterdämmerung. The dogs had not accepted me. Their hair, and mine, stood on end. I had my back to the wall.

'Ow-koy,' said the woman of the house, at last. A small light went on in the passage. We agreed the price – and that beggars can't be choosers.

Then we mounted the stairs. The room at the top presented a choice of beds. There was a spare mattress, which I helped the landlady to lift off the larger bed so that she could 'put the blanket on'.

'Ow-koy?'

'Yes, thanks.'

'Oi think yow'll be awlroight.'

'I expect so,' I told myself, nervously examining the door which she had left ajar. It had no lock. The dim light at the top of the stairs showed the bathroom, equally open and public, opposite.

I retreated to my bed. It was sensationally damp. The electric blanket did not appear to be on. I tried the alternative of a two-way switch. It would take hours to dry out. I finger-tested the other, smaller bed. Equally damp – a choice, it seemed, between double or single pneumonia. I rooted a little further down in the bigger bed, and a lady's nightdress came to light. What should I do? Take it downstairs, or leave it on the side for the owner to claim later? How much later? I was damp with sleet and sweat. I decided to try and phone my wife.

There were lights fully on downstairs. If the bathroom was like the sand-and-water area at an infants school, the kitchen was like the Wendy house – all the shelves, tables and other available surfaces, including the floor, cluttered with packets and containers and items of cast-off clothing left where they fell.

I yoo-hooed my way to the living-room door.

'Coom in.'

'I er. . .'

'Coom awn in boy the foyah.'

Here were more items of clothing – inner and outer garments – of all genders, airing themselves on radiators round the room.

'Er, I won't ask if I can use your phone – I'd like a walk.' I swallowed hard on my evident fib.

'Loik a drink?'

'No thanks. I. . .'

'If it's a wawlk yer want, there's a phown box oop the rowd. Sit down er minit.'

I took an armchair by the fire, from which I now had a view of a gentleman on the sofa who looked like a Hereford bull.

'Where yer 'eddin' fer, then?' said the Hereford bull.

'For Wenlock Edge – well, Acton Burnell, actually.'

The yard of pump water came in.

'Owdja git ta Acton Burnell frum 'ere?'

'Ditton Priors, perhaps.'

'Now,' said the landlady, 'not Ditton Proyahs!'

'Bouldon, I'd say,' said the Hereford bull, 'an' straight over Brown Clee.'

The yard of pump water went out.

'To see to the lambs?' I surmised aloud.

'Now, the 'eel yows downt lamb till Oypreel.'

I couldn't make out whether the yard of pump water was the landlady's son or not.

'It's a noice walk oop to the phown box.'

'Ah, the kiosk's just up the road,' said the Hereford bull. 'But ya shoulda gone Bouldon way.' I did not tell him that I so nearly did.

'Er, what time can I have breakfast? I want to be away early.'

'Wotja call early?' (this from the comfortable sandy bull).

'About eight?'

'Oight! That'll be ownly seven. The clocks go on t'noight. Oi'll afta see. . .' She winked at the Hereford bull.

'Well, thanks – I would appreciate an early start.'

'Remember – straight over Brown Clee!' the Hereford bull roared after me.

The dogs barked in the passage. Sleet nipped at my face. I must not get cold and wet again, I thought. After a hundred yards or so, I retreated back to the house, the pandemonium of dogs in the passage, the pickle in the kitchen and the bathroom, the unlocked bedroom, the unaired bed.

I fell asleep, exhausted, warm, moist and mystified.

Next morning, through the bathroom window, I could still see those haunting Malvern Hills. I did not seem to have travelled far.

My feet, I noted, were marvellous; my knees not so good. It was nine o'clock, thanks to BST.

He that is down need fear no fall, I muttered to myself over my toast and marmalade. Then, with only my bee-line map still sodden in my pocket, the cold lick of frost on my face, a skittering of snow on the earth, I mounted – if not like an eagle at least like the buzzard that flies over Clee Hill. I had the world to myself, except for a chaffinch who, like me, was glad to be alive and free, and an exceptionally lively and free young lady who drove a rackety milk-float with abandon up the hill, left it perilously perched by some houses, plucked full bottles from their crates, replaced them with empties, and assured me I was on the right path: 'Go straight on up!'

Titterstone Clee offered electrification, tarmacadam and – at the top – 'Aerial Services', the radar installations which I christened the maths workshop of the gods. There were, too, many old and new homesteads – some sleepy and salubrious on this Sabbath morn – with views that stretched beyond the Severn almost as far as Birmingham. The people who lived up here appeared to have 'made it' – but not lost sight of their roots.

Tight security at the top meant less security for me. The tarmac road ran out. I leapt down into a bog. Even the sheep had deserted me now.

'With difficulty we guess even at things on earth, and laboriously find out what lies before our feet; and who has ever traced out what is in heaven?' (Wisdom of Solomon.) I know just how Solomon felt. But what did he know of bogs?

Eventually I came to gorse and sheep again, and little comforting rills which told me there was a river running near. The water plashed on stone instead of sulking in reed-domed hollows of peat. It was open and playful and free.

The sun came out and revealed a bridge, a road and a steepled church ahead. Cool waters and green pastures with lambs. . . .

It was Cleeton St Mary again! The Hereford bull had been right!

Reader, do not follow me. I'm lost. I still have to cross Brown Clee.


'Bouldon, is it?' I asked a man clutching his Sunday paper and walking his glad-to-be-alive dog.

Chaffy cheered me on, keeping close to me, while a pair of buzzards wheeled and dealed and reconnoitred overhead. Their mewing was as cold and high-speed as a dentist's drill. I came to a turning which turned out to be a trackway to a farm.

A lady, house-proud as any in *Under Milk Wood*, flapped a duster outside her front door and retreated with a crisp 'Yes' when I asked if this was the path to Brown Clee. It was later marked with the sign of the buzzard: the symbol of the Shropshire Way.

It was noon by my dead reckoning.

There is seldom any continuity in paths and bridleways. It is like walking on a tightrope, you can be as easily off as on. And when you're off, you're very off! But under the lordly leadership of the buzzard sign I felt safe, and Brown Clee was solid – so far.

At Blackford kiosk I phoned my cousin Roger who lives at Hookagate, my destination for tonight.

'I'll make it.'

'By seven?'

'Don't know, but I'll make it.' A short, affirmative conversation. Hope lay ahead.

Somewhere down there out of sight lay the elusive St Milburga and her well. Pilgrim, press on, I said. An easy lightness buoyed me up. I heard voices – human or angelic I knew not – ahead. The high sides of this sunken lane were brocaded with primroses. I sat down on a grassy bluff and let a party of men from Birmingham go by.

'Are there any more of you?' I asked.

'Yiss, ther's the loydies still to coom. Yowl eer thim lawfin befowr they arroive.'

My bank, cushioned with moss and clumps of primroses, was like a throne. I sat like Corydon eating a Mars Bar, while the would-be shepherdesses passed. I only caught three words of their conversation as they went billowing by: 'Loonch atta poob.'

Brown Clee is on the whole firm and dry. It has fire-break hurdles and bell pits – depressions in the ground like inverted pudding basins – where coal was mined for centuries. It also has aerials at the summit, but no maths workshop of the gods. From here you can look back at Titterstone, in outline like the nose and cockpit of an aeroplane. Big-brother Brown Clee is rather like a pair of elongated molehills: a couple of burfs, Clee Burf and Abdon Burf. Both are over 1700 feet. Titterstone has more homesteads, and therefore more untidiness. It has ponies. It has tight security. Brown Clee is more friendly and wild. And it has the most beautiful hill sheep.

How, I wonder, does an animal with its head down grazing know you are there? But it does. A pony with a shock of mane over its eyes sees you before it looks up. It starts away, then faces up to you. So do the mountain sheep. They swivel round, look up, then turn, then either stand their ground or run. The fleeces of the yearling lambs are as silky and fine and long as if they had been shampooed and combed out. They look blond in the sun. The mothers, to whom they still cling, are in-lamb; they too are small-eared and nimble and neat. Here on Brown Clee, they run along dried ledges of heath turf like surf waves at sea. They flow rather than run. Quick-witted as deer, they are perhaps even more graceful in their down-to-earth way. Sure-footed they have to be: and hard-bitten as the skin-flint turf on which they feed. It is marvellous how these sheep of the Clees, the Long Mynd and the Stiperstones survive terrible winters and perennially come again to shine like flowers in the spring.

How should I sign my pastoral, I wondered. Anon? Or Corydon? Sheep, shepherds and angels are generally anonymous. I left it at that and began the descent, by patchy bogland again. I stepped on a tuft of reed and, twenty feet away, tall grasses swayed threateningly.

But soon I dropped out of the Hill of Difficulty to reach plush celandine-carpeted Corve Dale's edge. Here at Abdon, sheep have longer legs, bigger ears and topknots on strong tawny faces, and they gaze straight at you with amber eyes. And who should I fall in with but the Secretary of the Clun Forest Sheep Society? He put me on the little road (not marked on an AA map) that led by Pye Brook's primrose-blazoned banks to Tugford, Holdgate, on to Stanton Long.

Stands the church clock at ten to three – and takes no note of BST. . . .

Just down the road from the village and church of Stanton Long is a bridge, a little sandstone bridge, comfortably coped and eminently sit-able-on. I could imagine Shropshire lads of Housman's time whiling away long Sunday evenings here, smoking and frustratedly stubbing the earth with their steel-capped boots, dying, no doubt, for adventure and life with a capital L. There was no one there but me; and I had to hurry on.

I stopped at stately Shipton Hall, home of the Mytton family, which, I had read in an old Shropshire directory, 'exhibits a beautiful specimen of the Elizabethan style of architecture'. The Myttons, I presume, have died out; their memorials were all around the quiet church. But the hall, set back from the road, in gardens where Andrew Marvell, Michael Drayton and Sir Philip Sidney might have found Fair Quiet, seems just as they left it.

I came to Brockton, where Madeleine lived – the girl who walked along Wenlock Edge with me in the summer of 1951. I sat on the bridge here, too, and wondered how time, like a river, snatches us up like sticks and floats us along together – transporting us perchance for a day, then leaves us, one caught in a bank here, one hurrying on to some form of perdition elsewhere. . . .

I was less happy on the Edge now than I was in 1951.

I was tired and alone. I descended to Hughley, shins and knees protesting at the drop. Kenley 4, Acton Burnell 5, 4, 3. . . .

It was growing dark now and I could no longer read my map. Perhaps I should have taken the Kenley turn? That way, however, lay a mostly uninhabited stretch of common land – wooded, hilly and given over to sheep. There ancient churches lay about in fields. Even in daylight, you needed a horse on terrain like that. Aching, hungry and dying for a drink, I had chosen what seemed the more open, straightforward, northerly route.

Open it certainly was. I seemed to be surrounded by fields. But Acton Burnell seemed to be getting no closer. The last two signposts still declared it three miles off.

It must by now be seven o'clock and I had been asked for tea! I hoped they'd kept the kettle on. . .

At last, I reached the familiar long straight village street and there was my friend Rob Morgan hailing me from the gateway of Home Farm.

'Where've you been? Come in!'

There they all were in the sitting room – Tim and Sylvia Morgan, six of their seven children and two young friends, beside a blazing fire, their laughing eyes welcoming ME!

'You came a long way round,' said Rob.


At half-past seven, after tea and cake, we sallied out to see the sheep, by pick-up and the light of a thousand stars.

'It's a treat for us to see them again like this,' said Becky who is the shepherdess, 'remembering the dark nights in January when the lambs were mostly born.'

On a ridge, the exposed roots of an ash tree provided a stage for them to play on in the headlamps of the truck. Suffolks, they all looked like Frank Bruno to me.

'I'll take you to Hookagate,' said Rob. By winding lanes, lit by the steady stars and moon and suddenly swept by the beams of headlamps from his car he delivered me to Hookagate where my cousin Roger pitched me into the pub for a meal with his family. It was nine p.m. I had a day of rest ahead.

# Most roads
# lead men homewards . .

Here in the bosom of my family I rested, as completely as a man of my impatience and locomotive power can rest. There is, as thousands of summer visitors to farms will testify, nothing quite like farm hospitality. Work for the farmer and his wife never stops; but it is done, as it were, in season – in God's good time. They are not clock-watchers, they cannot be hurried; and you cannot help – indeed you had better keep out of the way.

Two perennial images dwelt in my mind as I lay in bed in the Great Chamber of this late-Georgian-style house, reflecting on life. One was of sheep and their lambs grouped under a pear tree in full flower in the orchard, still lying down, the lambs heads upturned to the sun, kissed as it were, by his beams. The other was of a hen, so busy last evening she must have stayed out all night, still trafficking after worms. She was shunting to and fro, forward and back, like a small locomotive on the same piece of track. She scratched and ran on, dipped, pecked, reversed and scratched again.

Called out of bed by birdsong and the sun's bright beams, I watched and wondered about these two ways of life for fully five minutes, then went back to bed. Thesis and antithesis, I thought: I might evolve a synthesis! A poet once saw the whole world in a grain of sand. . . .

Roger and his son David were already milking the cows. Ann would be feeding the calves. Roger who is large, laughing and loquacious has already handed over the running of the farm to David who is up with modern techniques, but his father's energy and good humour are – as much as his experience – indispensable. Ann, small, smiling and circumspect, is matron not only to the calves but to her children and grandchildren. She is churchwarden as well. She is into terriers and graveyard inventories: the Story Book of England. Roger has farmed here forty years; Ann or her family since 1916. And I, the itinerant schoolmaster, what have I to show for the harrowing years? The wheat stands still; the weeds move about.

Was it, I wondered, because I went to a school – the Priory in Shrewsbury – built on the site occupied earlier by St Austin friars, that I had become like a mendicant friar myself? What would life be like for me now if I had stayed at Little Ness? I sometimes envied the old woman whom Cobbett met at Ludgershall who had never been further than Marlborough – some twelve miles – and that only once. She was quite happy in her Wiltshire rut. And Cobbett discerned this in her face and settled state of mind. But what would he have been like if fate had attempted to pin him down? He left a book. The settled farmer leaves, as Emerson observed, 'a lump of mould the more'. But these 'earth-proud men' like Roger are farming not only for success but for succession; their goal is continuity. It seems that the people who make most stir in the world may merely be making waves.

The paradox of the nomad and the pilgrim is that we are constantly revising our life experiences. We have the consolation of going back in time – and almost seem to move ahead in time, just like that little hen. Clawed in, by classic skills, we scratch and scratch again the same small piece of ground.

The settled person is more like the sheep who really knows what's best for him: the grass is there, eat it; then lie under the pear tree and chew the cud. It is a misconception, put about by Isaiah, that 'all we like sheep have gone astray'. Men stray, yes; but sheep show much more sense. They have not our aggression or lust for land. They do not fight wars; and when they get a bit of good pasture they, by grazing and treading and manuring, invariably improve it.

Only a shepherd, in fullest understanding of sheep, could have written: 'Be still and know that I am God.'

Thinking of my sheep and my hen, I concluded that it is not the length of the journey that counts or the amount of ground we cover but the prolonged, concentrated application put in.

My reverie was interrupted by Ann calling me for breakfast. I did hope she would go on telling me about the difficulty of listing the graves in the graveyard.

'The old graveyard was easy,' she had said last night. 'The new one is more difficult. People move about more now.'

God would have rested the seventh day; I, a mere man, weakened by six, would fain go on and tackle Clun. God made these mountains; I, well-shod, would do my bit to wear them down.

The world on Tuesday the twenty-seventh of March was crisp with hoar frost, new-minted, caught in the eye of a red sun peering over Shrewsbury, its cupola, column and sundry spires. Tears sprang in my eyes so that anyone going to work at this early hour must have thought: 'Poor old tramp, I wonder what hedge he slept under last night?' They wouldn't know that I had been invited to dinner this evening in Clun.

Annscroft's little houses were asleep, their blinds and curtains drawn, frozen in memory, frozen in time.

Two, in particular, interested me, the homes of dear friends in the past: one, on my right, appeared empty now, and one, on my left, had not changed outwardly at all. It is strange to pass a house where you once enjoyed good company, from which the hearth and heart have gone.

The road ahead is notoriously winding and hilly with

the bleak attraction that characterises old mining settlements. Primitive Methodist Chapel, 1870. Jehovah is our strength. Pulverbatch 3, Bishop's Castle 14. That's where I was heading. The Tankerville Arms was all lit up. Horses stood to attention ahead. Farm dogs and a cockerel ripped the PRIVATE ice-seal off the air and told of TRESPASSERS.

A turret on a curved roadside wall with six small arches, a tiny steeple and a weathercock kept me amused. I supposed some farmer had wanted it to be IMPOSING. A little wooden gate was set in the curved line of bricks below the turret, slightly to one side ... it really was quite impressive. O Lord, our Governors – by such small trinkets of architecture have men of substance sat up in the saddle and entertained the rest of us. The horses told it all. They were part of the establishment, always. Caer Caradoc lay ahead! What better sight?

This is a landscape that has changed but little in centuries. Only the ant-like men, busy and black, the mainly Methodist miners whom the Earl of Tankerville allowed to build their places of worship on his land, are gone. I passed an old labourer's cottage in which I could see an anglepoise lamp set over a technical drawing-board, where once a harmonium might have stood, 'Jerusalem the Golden' open on its music rest. A county surveyor probably lives there now, planning to move more men.

Hawthorns and solid holly hedges lined the steep hill road; they were 'backed off' like Mr Sinnett's sheep. Sun warmed me now; I could keep my hands out of my pouch. The fields however were still lacquered with frost. Sheep came into view. Curlew bubbled in my ear; bluetits and chaffinches flirted, engaged in mid-air, then flew away. There were oaks in regiments, quartered about these fields. It was parkland – almost. A man was taking exercise with his spaniel in the field by the road.

'Are those your sheep?' I asked.

'No.' He was wearing gloves.

'Oh, the oak and the ash and the bonny ivy tree,' I sang, with abandon.

Suffolks and Mules looked sheepish on my left. They baa-ed pathetically. The frost had chopped their breakfast off.

Laburnum, cherry, mahonia, forsythia, berberis and periwinkle crowded the cottage gardens. A proud and careful people lived here, I supposed – altogether tidier than those on Clee Hill.

Sun, like a spotlight through gauze, illumined the great church and wonderful green hills that guard and girdle quiet Pulverbatch.

At a corner children waited for their school bus. I decided to ask what they call the hill on the right. The bus, arriving, cut me off.

'Broom Hill,' one of the parents said.

A stream, sunlit and smiling as a child who doesn't have to go to school, played near my feet. I had a pee. Hereford cattle questioned my business by their brook. Back on the road, a chaffinch had died. One less playmate for me.

Church Pulverbatch, I remembered, was the home of Sukie Lawley, the witch-evangelist, who converted the parson's family to Methodism: a mischief that made me laugh. A woodpecker, yaffling joined in.

Bridges 4, Bishop's Castle 12. Count down to Clun.

Here hedges, blown as it were all one way, were clouded not by hoar frost but by roadstone dust. I sighted a curlew coming in to land, light-breasted, angle-poised. A chaffinch cheered me on up a hill which was keeping quiet about its height, bends concealing what lay ahead. Here, at the top of the hill, were more horses and a couple of crows' nests in the oaks – smaller now but still plentiful – that commanded the heights. A crow, all black and conquering, flew over. A real carrion crow – as big as a raven, almost.

Climbing Cothercott, we lost the hedges – Chaffy and I – and gained the gorse, wire fencing, iron gates and cattle grids – the latter taking the place of good oak gates to make life harder for those who like to lean and look, and easier for those who cannot stop.

On top of the world, I took a picture of people camping by an old croft with a square of cultivation like a handkerchief spread out, a very tall ash and a lake in the coombe. At the turn for Habberley I saw the Devil's Chair – quartzite grinders in the maw of the Stiperstones. I hurried on to Leasowes Farm, ringed by beeches, like a royal coronet atop the hill, dipped down to Ratlinghope – ducks on a pond, a collie, a kitten and Kerry ewes at Lower Stitt Farm, where I saw my first plough-land, a quite extensive strip for potatoes, I guessed. Sycamore, alder, birch with catkins bright – and hornbeam again – luxuriated in this good-bottomed valley land. A buzzard wheeled and hung like a feathered boomerang, threatening the pleading peewit and snipe.

Eight lambs lay in a gully, tiny snips of things – one perched on its mother's back. Oh, the sunlit stream, the bonny Onny! No set aside here! That flitch of plough-land, south facing, well watered and well lit was the best I'd seen since the tawny field in the Cotswolds that reminded me of the walls of Jerusalem. Here the river was stiff with hazel and oak. Sheep were as big as young cattle. When did I last see a man?

There have been men about. Another Methodist chapel told me that. A well-laid hedge was quickly leafing out. A wayside rill, sunlit still, took its fill from a rocky hill. At the base of a deep-shelving quarried cliff was a bridge erected, it said, 1880: Thos Groves, County Surveyor, Coalbrookdale Co. makers.

Bridge time is reflection time.

I bathed with a girl-friend once by one of these Onnyside fields: got my wild oats wet. Came here then by bike, later by car, now by foot. . . .

A police car. Murder at the Gatten? Embezzlement at the Bog? Walking due south, the sun on my face, I felt light-hearted, free – 'the road before me. . .'

At one farm I passed some of Pharaoh's lean kine, one particularly wretched-looking cow pulled down, it seemed, by a boisterous, bonny calf. Holly, blackthorn, less oak, rushy meadows, rock humping up out of river and fields . . . remains of an old cottage. Caravans!

I came to Norbury and lambs with closed eyes, ears laid back, muzzles tipped to the sun. Few daffodils. Sheep looking dead were asleep: like cat, like horse. Stone gateposts, cement-rendered walls. The Mores' estate? A great solid C.P. school like a fort, a safe stronghold of no-nonsense learning, with a tower to put naughty boys in, stood in the middle of nowhere by the road. Where did the children come from? If any were still alive?

Gateposts round here were whole trees. How did men sink them? I couldn't get my arms round one.

The Sun Inn (Free House) proclaimed itself eleventh century – if so, I was sixteen. I fell in with hikers from Lancashire on a works' holiday. Fortified and free again, I studied a curlew landing on plough-land, in the sun. It was all potatoes now – all the way to Clun; tractors applying nitrogen, seagulls following, dipping and squealing, the men lonely in the cabs. There were sheep, of course, for company. Here, more than anywhere, I felt that sheep saved the landscape. They were not the tall Clun Forest sheep I had seen at Abdon, with amber eyes, darkie topknot, elegant duskiness and Ella Fitzgerald voice. These were the commercial Mule-crossed-Suffolk, seen all over England now.

Here, in a deep defile of the Onny Valley I was entering another country now, not England, not Wales. Here the hills, rough-coated as bison, are black with conifers. It was a darker world – a darker age, perhaps – which first made itself felt at Norbury where the little church – dark and cold – was sandwiched between the Sun Inn and the farm. It was like a candle snuffed out. Yews darkened its small space, and the farm backed on it with its black plastic bales and sheet-iron sheds. I experienced a sense of unease all along this valley: a certain loss of harmony.

Earth's music still had its melodies: the orange flush of a kestrel hovering; the church by the riverside, peeping through trees; wild duck winging; an old fallen ash, so hollow you could see right through it; the Ovaltine tilth of the fields; dandelions; the watchdog geese by a small farm's gate.

'Welcome to Bishop's Castle,' the notice said, but I took no heed – I was heading straight for Clun.


Surrounded by hills, Clun has 'old' written all over it. Its cracked castle keep is trussed and banded with iron; its ironstone church has no golden mellowness, no pillars leaning out, no bendy spire. It was built for defence: by small dark men who were busy outwitting smaller, darker men from the other side of the Dyke. Similarly, the bridge was designed to thwart rather than to let men pass. The visitor senses that he is still regarded with suspicion – an attitude which harks back to days when a visitor *was* an invader (and sometimes still is).

I sat in the castle grounds, that glowing late March afternoon, trying to sum the place up. I had not seen much of it yet. A notice in the market place told me that the Choral Society was still doing *From Olivet to Calvary*, John Henry Maunder's old Good Friday piece, tailored for Victorians. I thought of the words spoken by the Vice-Principal of the teachers' training college: 'Only through the Calvary of Sacrifice is the New Jerusalem to be achieved.' The war memorial outside the church listed sixteen dead in both world wars, mostly men of the King's Shropshire Light Infantry. Housman came unbidden to mind: 'None that go return', and 'The lads that will never be old'.

You cannot keep Housman out of your mind in Clun. This, more than Ludlow or Bredon, is a town marked out for war – a Sleepy Hollow, locked in on itself. You could easily imagine those lovely lads, hearing the drums of morning, crying 'Who'll beyond the hills away?'

A copy of the *Sun* lay on the grass. A headline caught my eye. 'WHY CAN'T MY DAD SEE I'VE GROWN UP?' 'Because he reads the *Sun*,' I wanted to reply. Only the jackdaws flying in and out of the keep would have heard me. I was alone with my diary and my thoughts and my elegiac mood.

'Clun is Conservative, within and without,' I wrote – jotting down words in the haphazard, hopeful way that jackdaws were dropping nest sticks into the hollows of the keep. There's a parable there, I thought: the bigger the hole, the more hope – and help – you need. '. . . as Conservative as the stone with which it is built,' I continued . . . 'a stone that is the colour of sand darkened by blood.'

The riverside fields I had seen before the last exhausting uphill trudge into town, lay to my left like wet chocolate, ridged by the plough. Wherever there was a flat-bottomed field there was a flat-bottomed trailer bringing Pentland seed potatoes in. Wherever there was a hill there were sheep: well-fleeced foragers who had grown in numbers in the last century to such an extent that a new market town, Craven Arms, had had to be built.

Clun, you see, is a backwater, off the main road and rail routes. Clun shrugs off the present, under its heavy black cloak of trees, and gets on with 'Olivet to Calvary'.

I felt a slight chill in my bones, sitting there scribbling – and forming no more satisfactory impression of Clun than the jackdaws were making of their nest. Perhaps less. Dry, cracked and crumbling, the castle is declared unsafe for humans, so Keep Out notices abound. Lord Clun, I was told in the town, finds it too costly to keep up. What, I wondered, did the townspeople think of this left-over giant's sandcastle, now a liability beyond defence? To have asked the question out loud might have been more like dropping a brick than a stick.

I carried these doubts in my head when I sat down to dinner that night. My host was a retired oil engineer, churchwarden and staunch Conservative; his wife an excellent cook. The other guests were the president of the Suffolk Sheep Society, a veteran local Conservative councillor and their wives. We talked about sheep and farming in general, the Gulf and North Sea oil, the nouveaux riches, and John Osborne who had settled dangerously close to town. These people were not latent Conservatives like me. They were good at accounts, sat on committees – nay, formed them. They supported the appeal to save the local hospital at Bishop's Castle. They were interested in their local schools. (Clun, I was surprised to learn, had no secondary school; its children transferred to a new one at Bishop's Castle.) Whatever was left of old Clun, they defended. They were proud of their town and were active in promoting its interests. Cobbett would have rejoiced, Blake would have gone to bed with a new vision of Jerusalem, and Tom Paine would have fled to America. I, in the midst of all this fine company, displayed, I hope, a certain elegant duskiness, went to bed and lay awake.

Good food, unfortunately, gives me indigestion.

Three images persisted in my mind, round which my dyspeptic thoughts formed parables: the little Hookagate hen, the all-prevailing sheep, and now those persistent, cackling jackdaws setting up house in the castle keep.

If animals were political, it was easy to see which party the hard-working hen would belong to. Without exactly adding acre to acre or field to field, she had an obviously Conservative bent, her lawyer's deeds would be sound, her accounts, at the end of the day, well totted up. There must be many like her in Clun. Then those old-style Whigs, the sheep. They represented the majority of cud-chewing middle-class England: opportunist yes, but without making much outward show, certainly not by scratching. As for the improvident jackdaws – well, they commanded a lot of attention, picking up benefits here (a bit of stray sheep's wool, perhaps) and allowances there (free rent of a castle). They were the real *hoi polloi*.

And then there was a fourth image: that of PLASSEY spelt out by the trees on the hill above Clun. It is said that Lord Clive had them planted there before he died – a disappointed, suicidal man. But this landmark was removed in the second world war, the trees cut down, because they might have helped enemy aircraft to get their bearings.

What did I know of Clive apart from his brief appearance in history notes at school? Plassey (in its time as famous a victory as Crécy or Blenheim) was the village in Bengal where he defeated Surag ud Daula in 1757 to avenge the Black Hole of Calcutta and deliver Bengal into British hands. What a turn up for the books, and for the young adventurer who had gone out as a clerk in the East India Company, discarded his pen, buckled on a sword and added not acre to acre but state to state, beating the nawabs at their own game.

Clive's statue stands in the market square at Shrewsbury: a proud figure in Ramillies wig, his frock-coat parted to reveal his high stomach, sash, sword and sturdy legs, one lace-frilled hand tucked into his beefy midriff, the other brandishing a charter – of fiefdom, not freedom, no doubt. Freedom, independence, leisure, can rarely have entered Clive's vocabulary. No flies on him – as Bill Sinnett might have said: he could catch pigeons! And, as a schoolboy, he had been playing ducks and drakes in the river when he remembered seeing, on an earlier ascent of the church tower, a flat skimmer ideal for the game, lodged in the mouth of a dragon, one of the gargoyles round the tower. He had to get that stone. A nation held its breath!

Clive, I supposed, was a born gambler. He went all out to win. Fame, money, corruption, cowardice – and all hell let loose on the battlefield – he had seen it all. Like all men of vision and exceptional energy, he could only experience his last days as an anti-climax.

It occurred to me that while Clive was lording it in India, Wordsworth, Cobbett and Paine had been writing libertarian tracts at home, or in treacherous France and America. Clive might have thought the words 'Churlish, thwart and mutinous' which Francis Bacon chose to describe ignorant men, too good for them.

Is it, I wondered, the fate of all extraordinary men – whether of action or of thought – to suffer disappointment in the end? Einstein's failure to resolve his Grand Unified Theory – more than the misuse of nuclear power – must have clouded his last years. Darwin, similarly, sought anxiously the unification of thought about Life and its origins on earth. Newman and Wesley, though travelling by opposite routes, longed for the same goal: Christ's vision of the kingdom of God on earth. The men with the really Big Ideas were unappreciated, it seemed, because we, the common ruck of people, viewed them from so far below.

I fell at last into the arms of Morpheus. And dreamed.

There on the castle ramparts, on makeshift builder's planks and scaffolding, stood Clive, a quill in his hand, writing PLASSEY on the cover of his grammar-school exercise book.

'It's my new play,' he said.

He was addressing someone bearded and old, who nevertheless wore a sword and looked like John Osborne.

'It would not be good for us all to live at Sandringham,' said the latter.

'Too stuffy,' said Clive.

'The world is well lost,' said Osborne.

'It is better to trust in the Lord than to put any confidence in princes: Psalm 118,' said Clive.

'I hear the drums of morning,' said Osborne. 'Who'll beyond the hills away?'

'Who said that?' asked Clive.

'Some twerp called Housman,' Osborne replied.

'Has anyone ever said anything that hasn't been said before?' asked Clive.

'I did,' said Osborne.

'What was that?' asked Clive.

'Look back in anger,' said Osborne.

'I do that all the time,' said Clive.

Leaving Clun next morning, I spoke to a bright, clean youth going to catch the school bus from the square. Two miles and two buses later, I saw two farm lads waiting for the school bus.

'Have you seen a bus?' asked the younger.

'I've seen three.'

'Brilliant,' said the older.

'You could try walking,' I smiled.

'We'll wait another two minutes,' they said, half-heart-edly.

Hitching up my haversack, I thought of Housman again:

> *He carries his griefs on a shoulder*
> *That handselled them long before.*

It must always be a problem to drive farm boys out of their Sleepy Hollows and push them into the wider world. They would rather work ten times as hard at home.

Bishop's Castle 4. That's a dolly for me, I thought. The dark chocolate fields turned to Ovaltine again.

B.C. stood proud and confident upon its hill. 'The Lord is in his temple; let all the earth keep silence before him. Habbakuk 2: 20.' The rooks, in the pines round the church, disobeyed.

STONE HOUSE HOSPITAL: BIGGEST DEMO YET, Church Street, Union Street and Station Street all carried notices proclaiming it.

POLITE POLICE PLEASE the great market hall declared.

There an old schoolfriend joined me, accoutred, map in hand, lovely old Brian Taylor with whom I first went on a jaunt – round the Horseshoe Pass, some seventy miles, when I was twelve. Brian, still boyish, in shorts and home-knitwear, sound boots and girdled with binoculars, is proof that age is only relative: a process of moving from field to field – each anniversary another gate passed through. He had it all worked out. We drove to Snead at the bottom of Corndon hill where he left the car so that he could walk a certain way with me; then, after parting, he would circle the hill, returning to his car. We passed farms quarried out of rock, painted, trim and spotless. No wasteland

98

here, except perhaps on the hill. Dogs slid out and in, keeping low to the ground. One poured like a black and white waterfall over a garden wall.

I should have said that the houses and gardens are quarried out of rock, with steps of exquisite artistry. There is maximization of space at Simon's Castle. Simon lived before the motor car.

We tramped round the hill, to the bat-boxes, chiffchaffs and buzzards of Roundfort Nature Reserve. Then leaned our backs against a gate to eat our lunch.

Gates. They were our assembly points when we were young. 'Keep nix!' They were something solid to hold onto in a mystical, expanding universe. They led to apples and to other stolen fruit. You could swing on them. Sometimes they reared and bucked you off. But best we loved leaning on them, forward or back.

Brian gave me some of his sandwiches: bread that was little different from that which his mother had provided fifty years before. He had half a Mars Bar and an apple from me: the oldest sacrament on earth.

I solo-ed on to Rorrington, and the stone circle with transcendent views of Long Mountain to the west – no wonder early man built for permanence in places like this.

I met a man who had worked for over fifty years on the Wakeman Estate.

'I'd do it all again, if I had my health and strength,' he said.

The extraordinary thing was that the Wakemans' great house – a kind of Edwardian pleasure dome – had completely disappeared. There was little even of the foundations left. There were groups of trees, many of them planted by the old man himself, and vestiges of the old tennis courts. He pointed out where the gun room used to be, the stables round the back, and where the coal was kept. But of the house itself nothing remained. He could remember it so vividly he could even project it to me, as if by some magic lantern of the mind.

The workmen's houses have remained undisturbed, uniformly attractive, black and white, with ochre and green lichened roofs of slate: colours that would have delighted Cézanne.

It was food for thought on the long, steep climb to Long Mountain. My chaffinch was still full of spink, among the ash groves and blackbirds of Wales. There was a place called Arcadia. A few people spoke with Birmingham accents. But it really began to *feel* like Wales. Even a parliament of rooks seemed to have picked up the lilt. Sheep grew smaller, dotting the steep-stepped side of the hill and checking their whippety, over-bold lambs. The carcase of a ewe lay half-stripped of its wool in the stream.

I picked up my feet. 'I walk like a king – penguin!' I cried, to the rooks, to the lambs, to Chaffy and all who could hear.

Two lads from Welshpool gave me a lift up the last steep hill to Harpwoods, my cousin Bob's bungalow on the top of Long Mountain.

'We'll pop you down to Welshpool,' he said.

After bacon and egg tea, I was delivered to my sister Joyce's house, and the customary steam-bath and traveller's tales.

# Green Valleys of Wales

On Thursday the twenty-ninth of March, I elbowed further into Wales. One of the places on my route was actually called Cefn-y-braich: the ridge on the elbow. It was a fine, clear morning, the ninth in a row.

'You're lucky with the weather,' my sister said. 'You'll go by Groes-llwyd on the Llanfair-Caereinion road,' she added, with Celtic confidence. I passed many Crosses on my way to Trefnanney, my first stop.

It was one of the best days of my life. Walking into the west, my shadow strode before me: tall, big-eared and long in the back – straight, too, if it had not been for my haversack, enlarged out of all proportion by the laughing sun. I could fancy myself seventeen again, my hair a dark cumulus cloud, untouched by time. There is nothing like your shadow on a bright day to make you feel young, unless it be Welsh air and ash groves and blackbirds singing, and hills and hollows, and sudden twists of a shiny, blue-steel road.

Everything this morning seemed designed to amuse. There was a good-humoured welcome abroad: in the notices pinned on trees inviting me to a pottery class, a coffee morning, an evening of flower arranging; in the busy black hen that scuffled to and fro in a field, her pattern of harrowing a tiny piece of earth the same as that of the Hookagate hen, and others like her for centuries; in the keen-eyed, friendly collie at the gate; the lamb that, startled, squatted and peed, then dashed off to its dam. These were not the little quick-witted, swivel-turn sheep of the Clees, but well-grown Cheviots, with fine heads and proud looks. They were white and clean, walking on smooth carpets of grass. For my valley was green.

This is the big surprise: Wales, far from being our poor

101

relation, is farming better than stuffy old England. There is a tendency, a tradition rather, to suppose that we English have the best of everything: in education (where are the Welsh public schools?), in church affairs (the grand old C of E), in politics (the Mother of Parliaments), in literature (Shakespeare), in music (Elgar), in art (Constable); above all, in land (set aside!) But England has become fossilized, so set is she in her ways. We forget that Shakespeare was familiar with Welsh, as his *Henry IV* testifies; that Elgar wrote his Introduction and Allegro for Strings after hearing the sound of singing above Llangranog, 'on a cliff, between blue sea and blue sky'. The songs, he wrote, were too far away to reach him distinctly, but gave him what he fondly regarded as 'the real Welsh idiom'.

It was that 'real Welsh idiom' that I caught so powerfully on my walk. This, it is true, was the fertile valley of the Tanat, flowing into the Vyrnwy (I think) and somehow embracing the Cain and the Rhaeadr as well. It was full of sheep, some stationed with their lambs on steep but smooth hillsides, some resting under trees.

'Go to Llanfyllin lamb market in June,' said Glyn at Trefnanney, 'if you want to see sheep, penned in a field with the old wooden hurdles, the butchers already sharpening their knives.' That frightened me off.

Lake Vyrnwy, Bala, Bwlch-y-cibau, the signpost said. Roadside laurels were in flower, primroses, cherry and – that darling of the early-morning sun – the gold, enamelled celandine. Constable would have given his eye-teeth to have seen them. For the ash lets in and filters out the light, better than most trees in its lacy, early-girlhood days.

I stopped by the lych-gate at Bwlch-y-cibau church. 'Heaviness may endure for a night but joy cometh in the morning,' I read. There was a zinc cup chained to a drinking fountain near by. '*Diolch*,' I said, in my best workaday Welsh. Lambs and two old ewes assembled round the base of an oak in the park. Playschool, I thought, and carried on. Free-range eggs, potatoes, hay and straw shavings were offered at the next farm gate. This was the lush Cain Valley – so lush, the people needed a high-fibre diet, perhaps. I passed a great place – a mill maybe? – with red dragons posted all over the walls. How many windows, I wondered, did it have? A hundred or more. I asked about it up the road.

'Was a workhouse, then an old folks' home, then a Challenge Centre – now they're talking of turning it into first-time buyers' flats.'

I called in at the Spar store for apples and a packet of 'picnic' Mars Bars. Seeing my haul and the haversack on my back, the lady at the till said: 'Going far?'

'To Llanrhaeadr.'

'It's a long way. I'll give you a lift in my car if you wait till five o'clock.'

'*Diolch*,' I said, and smiled sheepishly.

At Brithdir I found a church and a farm. 'Still used?' I called to a white-haired man sawing wood.

'Yes, yes – I'm glad to say. Yes, indeed, we're quite strong.' He came over to me, a smiling, graceful, beautifully-spoken old man.

When I reached Llanrhaeadr, the vicar – a lady – confirmed this. The church at Brithdir was one of the best in her group.

Llanrhaeadr, blessed place! My Alpha and my Omega!

The waterfall at Llanrhaeadr was, to us children at Little Ness, more than one of the seven wonders of Wales. Tan-y-Pistyll – the house under the fall – was the home of Ellen, one of our favourite aunts. She was born there, one

103

of six children of Ted Humphreys, a great shepherd, and still a legend in these hills. There are at home two pictures which keep for me his memory green. One is of Ted seated in his high-backed chair by the fireside, an Aladdin lamp lighting the page of a newspaper held between steady hands – significantly, his glasses are placed on the table beside the lamp. Is that his Sunday suit he's wearing to read the paper? Viewed in profile, you cannot tell. What thoughts lie behind those seemingly detached, unseeing eyes? He didn't, you feel sure, pose for that picture. The oil lamp, while keeping the paper intriguingly blurred, highlights his hands and his magnificent head. They are the hands of an honest and hard-working man. They have handled many thousands of sheep. They are gentle and firm, and so is the head. The nose and the ear jut out, as if on the alert. The mouth and chin suggest self-control. The brow is broad and high. The cranium holds brains.

It is a classic photograph, black and white, and timeless as some of the early Fox Talbots are.

I write at length about this influential image of my childhood, because it stands for permanence. It also perfectly epitomizes my theme. For Ted was a farmer, and also a member and warden of Llanrhaeadr church.

The second picture, taken about the same time, is of Eddie his son, then about fourteen, helping to bring the newly shorn sheep off the hill. The men have shed their coats too, carrying them loose on their arms. Except that they are driving, not leading their flock, it is an almost biblical scene. The sheep are the ewes from which, next year, will spring more of those white and long-tailed lambs which, I always think, most resemble the Lamb of God in stained-glass windows seen in Little Ness and everywhere in Christendom.

Tired though I was, on this last stage of my journey, I felt the consolation of going forward in space and yet back in time: of the prospect of meeting people I have known, or seem to have known, all my life. It is a feeling of actually getting younger – one which pilgrims must have always felt as they reached their long-sought goal, especially that of the longest journey of all: the journey home. Is Heaven like this? The wind in the tubular gates by the roadside told me so.

No wonder my pace quickened as I reached Llanrhaeadr, my Beulahland, my Bethel in the hills. I did not hope to see Eddie; he would be shepherding or running his dogs at a trial somewhere. But I would see Ellen, my old Aunt Ellen's niece. And, on this occasion, I had an appointment with the vicar, a considerable coup, as it turned out.

Now everybody knows, since it was acknowledged even by the Royal Mail, that Bishop William Morgan of Llanrhaeadr and St Asaph first translated the Bible into Welsh. I was shown his house which is now a pigsty; and a point across the river where, in a summerhouse, he worked on his translations, lost to the world. In fact, the vicar told me, the parishioners complained that he did not give them more of his time.

*Plus ça change. . . .*

We went inside the church where an exhibition celebrating the quatro-centenary was still in place. The window's stained-glass represented, sure enough, the Good Shepherd and the little white Lamb of God.

A picture is worth a thousand words and I think it was at that moment I realized why Ted, in the photograph, did not need his glasses to read the ephemeral news of the day. He had the Good News in his head.

I thanked the vicar, blessed all kind friends, and went on my way.

On, on, by Ty-brith, I continued, with Llanarmon

Mynydd Mawr on my left. The sun smiled, motorists waved – just as the vicar had said they would – and I saw my finest ash tree yet: in the hollow of a field beside the road. I scrambled onto the hedge-bank to try to photograph it. Sheep darted away. That ash was like the burning bush! You could see why it was not consumed. It was inexhaustibly, spontaneously combustible!

The sun lighted on the blue Berwyns ahead. Hedges were ribbons of green shot-silk. The road wound on and on. Llansilin would not come. And where was Cefn y braich?

A car slowed down. Carys, my friend, picked me up. 'It's only a few yards,' she said.

She took me, after *bara brith* and *paned*, to Sycharth, home of Owain Glyndŵr. I had walked through five centuries! It was only a short step to Oswestry and home to Baschurch and Little Ness.

# The farms of home

I walked next morning to Little Ness, over fields where I first learned to walk. Baschurch is three miles from Little Ness where I lived till I was twenty-two. It was there, to the farm by the church, that I was heading now. It was from Church House that our mother led us – my brother, two sisters and I – quacking like a duck in French: '*Allez vous en – tout de suite!*' We followed like ducklings struggling to keep up, in close-order, no questions allowed.

Our mother really walked like a duck, single-mindedly heading her brood. She brooked no deviation to left or to right; but she did allow us to stop by the river at Milford bridge.

It must have been there that I developed a taste for reflection, or 'dreaming' as it was called.

That sandstone bridge! On sunny days like this, when grass was long but not yet turning into hay, we would pick a roadside piece to suck as old men sucked their pipes. We draped our bodies over the warm parapeted bridge, and talked and mused and mused and talked. We would watch fish flicker in the water below, which was always clear at Milford, sunbeam-spotted, flashing on numberless pebbles and flints, speckled – white, pink and roan. We talked from down below our knees, our heads hanging down, arms hugging the friendly stone. We would pitch little fingerfuls of moss and lichen into the water or at each other. A breeze shivered on our shins and I would drift with my dream into worlds unknown. The river had wrought its power on me.

'Cooee! We can't stay here all day!' What Mother had been doing while her ducklings idled, I cannot say. She called at a cottage, perhaps. She never could rest in the day.

And if she wanted to go further afield, we went open-mouthed by pony and trap. At one lift of the reins, the black pony would fly. 'Close your mouth, Peter, and do try to breathe through your nose!'

It was with thoughts of Mother that I occupied my mind on this lovely March morning, so sunny it was more like summer than spring. How she would have enjoyed those hedges heaped with may! The cottages still had gardens that, being near the river, were loamier, lighter and earlier than ours at Little Ness. Ahead were the magpie timbers of Milford Hall, where Humphrey Kynaston, the highwayman, was supposed to have hidden, then jumped from a window straight onto his horse before dawn and the Law arrived. It was newly restored, standing like a Tudor matriarch out in the sun, in apron of daffodils and bonnet of pear blossom – a beaming, welcoming, enduring sight.

Up Milford bank we walked – my mother, two sisters, my brother and I – then struck over the fields: those fields which were always a pattern of husbandry. No set-aside here! The hedges and ditches were cut and cleared. The land looked clean, and in good heart. Tidiness is the hallmark of good farming, and this Red House land was never left to go rough. Secluded Adcote smiled in the sun. It always did. It is where the Darbys built their magnificent sandstone hall which has been for many years a private school for girls. It is bowered by trees. No prick-eared hunters proudly paced the park, but butter-fat Charolais steers were industriously putting on weight. Somewhere behind all those cedars and rhododendrons a well-bred young lady may yet have been declining *fluvius* while the River Perry flowed unheeded and unheeding by.

As a young boy at church, I had misplaced sympathy amounting to love for those pale Adcote girls who at Holy Eucharist went down like nine pins in faints. They were helped out to the porch, staggering, by po-faced mistresses, a glass of water rushed after them. I would fain have helped, but could not leave off blowing the organ for fear of its running out of wind.

When I asked my mother what was the matter, she said; 'Growing pains!'


I cut across to the church. Here the lane leads to World's End: an altogether different secluded state. That was where we went, the boys of the village, when we wanted to be private.

And here in the graveyard there is absolute peace.

As usual, this happy Resurrection time, I tidied Mother's and Father's graves, not wanting to be caught out. There is little that will grow on this cold East side. But the sun puts fresh heart into things bitten off by the wind: heathers and aubretia and saxifrage. Cut flowers in pots stand no chance.

I turned to admire, as always, the Patches, the Leasowes – the riverside fields, smooth as green baize with good-sized trees and contented cattle, Friesians black and white, as fresh as paint, like figures on a large-scale model farm.

Then I walked round to the west. There lay our old place, sunk in decay, the slates nearly all off the barns, the fields all left to go rough. There were no animals to give it even a semblance of life. Why? I had not the heart to enquire. The church, as always now, was locked.

# PART THREE

# TIME FOR AMENDMENT

# Forth I wander, forth I must

Two years and two months later – restless, long-lived dragonfly that I am – I took off again. I went, this time, by car; not the sporty green MG of my early motoring career, but the solid blue Volvo designed to prolong my retirement to the limit. I wanted to be sure to return.

My mission was more complex, more wide-ranging than before. I wanted a bigger overview. By car, I thought, I could better employ my compound historical eye.

Walking, you tend to take an undeviating route: the line of least resistance, so to speak, from A to B. Driving, you make more detours, voluntary or enforced. Walking, you make the most simple connections. By car, you can zigzag about. (See back endpaper.) This time I had no bee-line map. I wanted to see places I had visited before, but I also hoped to see others unknown or only heard or dreamed about. I wanted to follow my instinct, with whatever happy improvisations providence might throw in my way.

This time, I decided, I would not fail to see the Uffington White Horse – unmissable one might think, but missed by me before.

I could not have done better had I gone by air.

It was ten to seven on Wantage church clock. Was I the first 'tourist' abroad? I had passed King Alfred's statue in the market-place, virtuous, white and imposing as ever. A few traders were setting out their stalls, whistling good-humouredly. Trucks rolled into the square. A man was sweeping out the forecourt of a pub. A paperboy,

113

fresh-faced, went on his rounds. If I were an industrialist, I thought, I would employ paperboys – especially those, like him, who walked. In the footsteps of Alfred, this one – who might have been a Latin scholar at King Alfred's school – was hauling his bag: luminous on the outside, more lurid within. He smiled. Bent on ridding himself early of all that Saturday trash – for which people actually paid – he smiled. Cars littered the streets and the back lanes of the town, scattered remains of Friday night. Better to walk, I imagine he thought. I stood my ground outside the great church, levelling my camera at it and trying to capture the striking tower, extended lead roof and jutting porch all with one shot. I noted that this Priory church is 'high': how high could be discerned from the presence of a Father among the clergy staff who put out a notice offering Family Mass. Why not? This is Alfred's town, not Henry VIII's.

Among the lilacs, laburnums and lesser celandines near Locks Lane I saw my paperboy again.

'Locks Lane?' I asked. 'Does that mean there's a canal?'

'Just a brook,' he said.

'What's its name?'

'Letcombe Brook.'

'Thanks.'

I hoped I would find a mill. I found a most peculiar bridge: a few planks with a notice saying THIS BRIDGE IS NOT DEDICATED AS PART OF A HIGHWAY AND THERE IS NO RIGHT OF WAY ACROSS IT. Playing fields lay beyond it, a housing estate backed onto them and a man on a bicycle whistled past me, apparently on his way to work. The mill house – if such it was – was drowned in sleep and may and cow-parsley. I beat it back to town. At the top of the street the paperboy had left his bag by the gate and gone into the big house. He moves with the Times, I thought. I returned to my car on the Uffington road.

I thought I would be alone on White Horse Hill, alone
with the sheep and the wind-blown lark. The morning
mist lay over the valley, concealing man's works below.
The sun, that showed me seven o'clock on Wantage church,
now shone on chalk pared over twenty-one hundred years
ago. Anonymous, this horse belongs to no one and to all
mankind. And this is the time to see it, I thought. Sheep
hardly bothered to get up as I fixed my eyes on the
landmark ahead. If they did they were butted by lambs,
three-quarters grown, that had to kneel, screw, swivel,
shunt and hoist their mothers off their legs to suck. Larks
sprang from the turf two paces ahead of my feet; turf which
is more than two thousand years old; firm and springy;
settled, yet rolling like the rising sea. How curved the earth
is in these parts! You are almost conscious of its spinning.
No wonder the larks are so restless! The Horse leans away,
his outline like some strange new continent etched on the
edge of a globe, one leg an island detached. And where is
his head? A notice says DO NOT ADVANCE BEYOND
THIS POINT. The ground is eroded near his head. People
have been standing – *are* standing – on his eye! I didn't see
them before. They didn't see me. They skulked away. The
wind cannot read.

The remains of the hill-top fort held no enchantment
for me now. I worried about those scuffings of the chalk,
which even the sheep must make sometimes, in their con-
stant nibbling and nourishing of this time-honoured turf.
Mostly it is like jute, uninvaded by dandelions or even
buttercups. It is cross-threaded by thyme, the secret of its
sweetness and its strength. Here and there another flower,
a darker blue, appeared like a tiny blob of ink – such as a
mapping pen might make. I did not know its name. But,
that morning, while the world was spinning into light I

stood 'outside myself', I did not want to know names. The earth was new. Adam and Eve had not spoilt it for me.

My mind was again running on sheep. It is not surprising that Blake and Palmer depicted them as creatures of a higher, better world. One sheep has no spirituality; yet, as flocks, they line the paths to Heaven. No other animal looks so at home on a hill. Oxford Down, Southdown, Cotswold, Kerry, Scottish Blackface and – most like the pure white lamb of Blake's imagining – the Welsh Mountain, all look as well on a hill as fantails on a dovecote roof. They catch, and hold the light.

The ewes on White Horse Hill were mostly Mules: Welsh and grey-faced Leicesters mixed. But their lambs were uniformly Downland to my eye: pig-eared, sandy-faced and double-chinned. I would have to ask.

Back down to earth, I called at a farm, rang a bell and received a response: 'Don't know. We're all arable 'ere. I 'ate sheep!' I would have to ask elsewhere. So much for my view of a small England with large horizons breeding large ideas!

I took a picture of a live white horse in a corral at Mill House Stud, in a Samuel Palmer may-and-coltsfoot setting, by a roan-brick house with white sash windows, oozing quality and pride. Looking into the sun, back south again, the White Horse on the hill still strode loose-leggedly, fantastically, two-dimensionally, against all probability. My live horse capered off.

Just as I was wondering where all the other horses were, I saw a lady snatch one, from a field of about twenty, to be shod – on the roadside. Cool operators, these blacksmiths. I stopped the car to take a photograph. Seeking permission, I said: 'I hope I don't obtrude.'

'Go ahead,' said the girl, shortening her arm and pulling the horse's head down. Short-backed, the blacksmith

116

trimmed the left hind foot. I could see how troublesome
to a blacksmith a long back would be. Arched and aproned,
his whole body was tucked into the horse. Could I send
them a copy? I asked.

'Send it to Dave,' the lady replied.

'What address?'

'David New, Longcot'll find me,' the blacksmith said.
No wasted energy there.

'Thanks,' I said, and bucked back to my car.

The land was now given over to oil seed rape. I had left
the indomitable Downs behind with their quiet sheep and
even quieter shepherds, their biddable horses and reticent
blacksmiths, their long unaltered natural outlines, their
welcome savageness. What for? Harsh ICI green of early
corn and cadmium yellow of *Brassica napus arvensis*. Only
the tender leafing-out of oak and the roadside procession
of cow-parsley consoled my eyes. I hate the forced onrush
of summer in our fields before spring has come of age: it is
like the loss of innocence in our children, over-developed
too soon. Rape: significant, unfortunate, outrageous, blas-
phemous word. Why not call it abuse?

I stopped by a beautiful old field gate, inviting to
lean on, I thought. It was small, old-fashioned, made of
oak. It too had had its day. No large machinery could
pass between its posts. Pedestrian passage was blocked by
refuse bags, an old fire-extinguisher, decaying carpets and
upholstery. I could not even pat my gate, stoutly resisting
submergence, but sadly beginning to lower its head. A
cuckoo called. O, word of fear! I moved on.

I came to Watchfield with its notices warning the public to keep out: a message reinforced by walls and looped
barbed wire. If it's ugly, I thought, it's for defence purposes. I spoke to a little old man, safe outside his retirement
bungalow. 'Ministry of Defence,' was all he could tell me,
taking his shopping and newspaper in.

117

Near Coleshill I spotted a man straining on a rope, another man high in the rigging of an aerial. Radar, I supposed. If I had stopped to speak, he might have lost concentration, the defence of the realm falling about our ears. Better to speak to a blacksmith with his feet on the ground.

Coleshill ahead, high on a hill, steep valley between, houses packed in, hand over hand, roof over roof, pitched and gabled, chimney-potted, tight-fitting, grey-gold in the sun. People here live on top of one another – Church-centred, it seems; happily cultivating and comparing their gardens. I stopped by the bridge. I was leaving the Borough of Thamesdown twinned with Salzgitter and Ocotal. A mallard in the River Cole was leaving me. Above the town I chased a hare; young, loopy, undefended, free.

At Buscot I almost fell into the arms of the National Trust. 'Almost', because on entering the long sweep of the drive, I spotted a Land Rover parked by the portico, gun dogs barking in the back. Thinking that the house would not be open at this early hour and that the dogs might not have had their breakfast, discretion got the better of me and I doubled back to the church, there to muse on memorials of pilgrims of old, more valient for truth than I.

Tucked under the wing of the estate, as it were, the little mediaeval church is a history lesson in itself.

Manorial, dark and weighed down with tombs and memorials, this provided the first of my diary entries under PATRONAGE to date:

### Bufcott August 17th 1801

Mrs NASH of Maidenhead (at the request of her late husband, Mr Thos Nash of London, Sugar refiner, son of Mr John and Mrs Elizabeth Nash of this parish) left in her will money to be laid out in the parish funds, the interest to be applied by the Church Warden and overseers in the annual purchase of 20 coats for 20 poor men and 20 gowns and petticoats for 20 poor women resident in this parish. £1166.13/4 at 3 per cent Reduced Annuities providing a yearly income of £35.

Were those the tombs of the family outside the church? If so, their names were erased by time. I looked in vain for any kind of man in a coat or woman in gown and petticoat.

I headed for Lechlade and its church and the table-tomb on which, two years and two months before, I had sat to eat my tea. I was anxious to see to whom I owed that mite of patronage. On the wall, alongside the walk to the graveyard, is a plaque which quotes lines from a poem 'A Summer Evening in Lechlade Churchyard 1815' by Shelley. I had not noticed before that this was Shelley's Walk. Old yews cast shade; old table-tombs – round-topped 'wool-pack tombs' – sank down, inviting me to do the same, most sittable-upon. Some, indeed, were breaking down, their inscriptions long, long gone. And so was that of my old host. I saluted him: *benedictus benedicat*.

I went inside the wonderfully light, expansive church whose inner doors – all polished wood – were 'placed here largely by the inspired thought and generous gift of Alf. King'.

I travelled on, by Macaroni Woods, bluebell-carpeted and coming into leaf. It was here that I first noticed how the ash varies this year. Here it is out, there it is not. Perhaps it depends on the height.

At Hatherop I found men at work, cutting and ferrying silage from the fields. It seemed a great estate. Jersey cattle, glossy as deer, paraded in the model park. If the Cotswolds began for me at Coleshill, here they reached their apogee. Wisteria overhung the house. May efflor-esced. Horse-chestnuts (also red and white) reared up.

119

The copper beech put on more girth, swelled purple with pride. But grass was king. For silkiness I had not seen, for savouriness I had not smelt such grass. The petted cattle grouped themselves in attitudes of bliss.

I ruminated on. I knew from a radio programme, that the Coln Valley had deep woods and nightingales. I had seen the Swan at Bibury, the old weavers' cottages at Arlington and the ice-cream-licking, litter-dropping crowds. Not there, could I hope with Shelley 'that death did hide from human sight sweet secrets!'

At Coln St Aldwyns I gazed up at the gable of the mill, on which I read:

SIR

MEHB

BART

1838

The owner of the house next door did not know what this meant; he had only been here two years. But a man, blessed with two MGs – one A, one B – at work in his garage explained:

'Sir Michael Hicks-Beach, Lord St Aldwyns, M.P.'

I thanked him. He also stressed that the cockpit of his MG A was 'all wrong'. It was red and the seats were plastic. It should be black and leather. He was stripping it out.

I told him how we used to drive down to the river to bathe, two of us in the seats and one in the dickie, towels tucked in by the tank.

'You wouldn't do it now!'

'Oh, that we looked after our rivers as you look after your cars!'

'Our mania for being clean has led to this,' he said, grubbing about among his oily tools.

At Coln Rogers I read in the church that twenty-five

men of the parish and one V.A.D. had gone to the First
World War and all had returned safely. I learned also that
the old priest's house was used, forty years ago, for
housing pigs. At Coln St Dennis I noted that, of the fifty
odd vicars who had ministered there, many did not stay
long. Between 1661 and 1793 there were seven Hugheses:
a certain familial stability set in; but Samuel Pitt Stockford
only stayed one year, and neither Lewis By-the-sea Bubb
nor his predecessor Robert Paul Bent laid down roots. ONE
GENERATION PASSETH AWAY AND ANOTHER COMETH
some wag had ordained should be written as a tailpiece to
the list. Precarious vicars of Christ!

Memorials in churches poignantly show how precarious, even for the good and the great, was their hold on
their titles and estates. Here in Coln St Dennis is a plaque
to Sir Benjamin Kemp, Bart., excellent scholar and honest
man, only son left of the numerous progeny of Sir Robert
Kemp, Bart., who had four wives and fifteen children. The
title descended to a cousin, and the estate to a neice (*sic*).
And so to Chedworth, on the eve of Pentecost.


If I were King, I would choose Chedworth for my capital.
Cedda knew a good thing when he chose it for his homestead. Among the deer antlers, arrowheads, horseshoes,
spurs, spoons and earthenware at the Roman Villa museum,
are three freestone slabs, on which are inscribed the Greek
letters χ and ρ, evidence, perhaps, that the builder was a
Christian. Another stone in this collection has the word
PRASIATA roughly chiselled on it. 'There was,' says
J. Arthur Gibbs in *A Cotswold Village*, 'a British king,
by name Prasutagus, said to have been a Christian, and
possibly it was this man who built the old house in the
midst of Chedworth woods.'

Gibbs is very good on mediaeval manor houses, too,

121

particularly the one described near the beginning of his lovely, affectionate book. Generalized though it is it perfectly conveys style: that of the manor and the man that built the place.

'As I walk down the road I come suddenly upon the manor house – the "big house" of the village. . . . Over the doorway of the porch is the following inscription. . . PLEAD . THOU . MY CAVSE ; OH . LORD.' It was 'long and somewhat low,' he says, and 'of some size'. He pushed open the 'solid oak door' and found himself in the hall. . . 'The old-fashioned furniture, the old oak, the grim portraits and quaint heraldry, all were there.' And he was 'much interested in some carved beams of black oak, which . . . originally formed part of the magnificent roof of the village church.'

Small wonder the builder asked the Lord to plead his cause! It puts me in mind of another inscription – this one over the door of a wool merchant's house:

> *I praise God and ever shall*
> *It is the sheep hath paid for it all.*

But to return to Chedworth, a perfect anthology of all things typical of the Cotswolds: a village clinging to the steep sides of a valley, the cottages appearing to grow out of it; water rushing out from the top of the hill and tumbling down the street; the high perpendicular church on the same hill to the east, golden at sunrise, bronze at sunset; old wrinkled lynchets on old manor fields, a mill pond, a pub. . . .

And, beyond the V of the village, to the east, is a high plateau; to the west are dense, dark woods.

On the high plateau are the airfield and the cricket ground: each offering opportunity for attack and defence. And I cannot think, if I were king, where I could find a better place to build my pleasure dome; to plot and plan and, in a clearing of those woods, to plant and store my provender; and build, perhaps, a planetarium. For there I could have the best of all worlds. I could watch the stars in their courses on clear nights and the full moon rise over the hill to the east. On dark, wet winter nights I could still put on my West End show, with chorus of owls and nightingales and giddy royal bats.

Another place tucked away and tantalising to me was Elkstone, extolled by Arthur Mee. He went in search of it between the wars. What better place to go in search of peace?

I had passed the sign which says Elkstone 1 on many a frenzied North/South run. That is how close the battling motorists on the busy A417 (old Ermin Street) come to nirvana – which my dictionary defines as the extinction of all passions and desires and attainment of perfect beatitude (Sanskrit for blowing out!).

I arrived full of pentecostal goodwill. It was a quarter past ten. A small congregation, which I joined, was advancing towards the west door of the church.

'Are you a ringer?' asked one – a man in shirt-sleeves. 'We want one more to make up the number.'

'I'm sorry,' I said. 'You'll have to blame my misspent youth!'

I think he said it was never too late to learn, but both he and I knew my moment of glory was gone.

I entered the church with heightened expectancy. There is nothing like a peal of bells or a blast of full diapason on the organ to bring a church to life.

Grey and gaunt without, it was suffused with light within. Beyond the low white chancel arch (Norman) the little sanctuary was bathed in an inviting amber glow. There was no artificial light, and little stained glass. Whence came then this supernatural light? It was Whitsunday morning. The church was decorated throughout with cow-parsley, creating a wild, supernatural effect. Nature here transcended art. I crept about, slack-jawed, amazed. No sound came from the ringers ascending the tall tower steps: a tower, the printed guide told me, which was a fine example of the workmanship of a local school of masons deriving their inspiration from Gloucester Cathedral. Nothing that it said about the chancel could explain that circumambient light. I crept about, ignoring all that the guidebook said I should see: the rare 'paterae', cusped niche, plain chamfered vaulting-ribs, the columbarium ... I was spellbound by the subtle secret of that light, so tantalizingly withheld from me. It was Blakeian: What immortal hand or eye! To know might be to break the spell. And then the bells rang out. . . .

Awed by Elkstone, I headed north east to Winchcombe, birthplace of Jack of Newbury. I wanted to see where this self-made fifteenth-century founder of one of the first industrial towns was raised. What special air had he breathed? What horizons beckoned him? What had bred in him such independence of spirit that when Henry VII offered him a knighthood he, John Winchcombe, begged to be excused the honour; he, who had been an apprentice clothier, who had married the merchant's widow, who owned all Northbrook Street and the woollen mills around, preferred to remain plain Jack, as he was known to his six hundred workers and everybody else in his adopted town. Winchcombe, I thought, must have given him a good start.

*En route*, I came to Whittington: by a way which took me down and up a hundred dumpling hills, covered as it were with custard in the form of sheep. I reached a plateau once more, perhaps a plain, straightforward as this ordinary looking church. But Arthur Mee had written in his *The King's England*: 'Together they stand, the great house and God's house, in company with a 14th century cross, a grand old yew tree, and the Moat which protects them both.' Ah, the temporal and the spiritual cohabiting again!

It was originally a Norman manor, and inside the church are the life-sized effigies of two knights believed to represent Richard de Crupes and his son, also named Richard, Lords of the Manor of Whittington. A third, the guidebook says, may represent the wife of one of the knights; and adds – supporting my theme of benevolent patronage – 'it has been said that for some years this family evidently loved and strove for the welfare of Whittington folk.' Perhaps, I could not help thinking, young John Winchcombe had learned something of them. Perhaps from a Whittington aunt. 'You know young Richard Whittington came from Coberley, not far from here. And *he* made good,' she might have said.

Between Whittington and Winchcombe, I found myself perched on the edge of Cleeve Hill. Perched, too, were great beech trees, their roots reaching onto the road. Hikers staggered; motorists slowed. The views were breathtaking: fast-changing, with bursts of electric oil-seed rape, watercolour washes of bluebell woods, foam-waves of cow-parsley, green oceans of corn, but hardly any sheep. After a few more corkscrew turns, the world was straightening out. Those careering down could now only envy the ones careering up. Perhaps it was this that motivated Jack?

His town I found flat: pinched, unabsorbing, uninspired. I could smile at the names of some of the houses in Gloucester Street, but the weavers' cottages and Cotswold House left me, and probably their owners, cold. Winch-

combe has two ancient inns, the George and the Corner Cupboard. But what do you make of the church?
*Concordia et industria* it says on the Old School near
by. No question, you would not be distracted by the
view from this end of town. The church completely blots
it out. It must have been built – in 1468, after Jack of
Newbury left – to stop the weavers seeing the flat, fertile
land toward Evesham, beckoning like the Promised Land.
It is a monstrous taker-up of space. Inside, a huge Flemish
candelabrum (brass) with real candles hangs halfway down
the high perpendicular nave. The whole building is marvel-
lously light. I counted ten windows on the north side alone.
Outside, I gave up counting on the gargoyle-grinning,
sun-struck south. For hugeness Winchcombe takes the
cake. After a few bites, I'd had enough.

In Bredon, my next stop, the tamarisk was out. Spired
and inspired, here, the church is tended by one David
Brown and his father, who – David told me – had worked
on that roof – and the spire whose top was blown askew
by the 1990 gale.

Bredon is, by any reckoning, superb. It was owned
in the past by the powerful Lord Bishops of Worcester, and boasts a mediaeval tithe barn grander, I think,
than Great Coxwell's. Almost as grand as the tithe barn
is the rectory with its extensive grounds and outbuildings
stretching nearly to the river down Dock Lane. I did not
go down that steep road nor did I go out to the hill. My
eye was fixed on that elegant, uplifting church.

Inside are many great monuments and fine furnishings,
but I made a note of two plaques in particular.

The first commemorates John Prideaux, 84th Bishop
of Worcester, 'a man of learning . . . driven from his see
in the Great Rebellion, who died in poverty at Bredon,
1650.' Born in Devon, Arthur Mee says, he looked back
in his poverty to his Devonshire days and, remembering

a petty appointment he had failed to gain in his youth, he would say, 'If I could but have been parish clerk of Ugborough, I had never been Bishop of Worcester.' Left with only a few shillings a week to live on, he sold his books and furniture to keep body and soul together. He is quoted as saying at the end, 'I have become an ostrich: I have eaten a great library of excellent books; I have eaten a great deal of linen, much of my brass, some of my pewter, and now am come to eat my iron, and what will come next I know not.' From under his cloak he showed a piece of iron he was taking to the smithy to sell for his dinner.

The second plaque commemorates Rector Prideaux Sutton (strange echo of names!) 'generous to his Domesticks, and a most desirable Companion . . . perfectly knowing how to maintain gravity without morofenefs, and mirth without levity.' If only I knew that, too!

I noticed on the war memorial in the church how many men of Bredon had joined the Royal Navy: evidence of a taste for boating early acquired on the river – and the whole area's traditional links with the sea. What memories, I wondered, did they take, those men of Bredon, on their ships overseas: the bells, the 'coloured counties' from the hill, the larks, the tamarisk in flower?

I had approached Bredon with caution, almost amounting to fear. Its sweet-sounding name, its association with Housman in his more melting moods, its outdoor reputation with the river and hill near by, had led me to believe – and not to believe.

But Bredon, by any reckoning, is superb.

# A fair field full of folk

On top of the world on the Malverns, my mind was coloured by the rapacity of those old princes of the Church, priors, abbots and bishops, who vied with one another for land, even threatening the king. They knew a good plot when they saw one. They ran sheep on the hills and fish in the rivers – and here there were plenty of both. As Lord Ernle said in *English Farming Past and Present*, 'They laid acre to acre, and field to field,' and 'They alone could offer an inviolable resting place for the dead.' Ay, there's the rub. For fear of the dark, read fear of death. It is easy to see how Alfred, Edward the Confessor and the boy king Edward VI attained the reputation of saints when compared to these leviathans of the Church. They made mammoth mediaeval takeover bids. They not only milked the sheep and the fish; they milked, with their tithes, the people as well. They really *farmed* the land, in the sense that they farmed it out. No wonder Langland and Bunyan dreamed and then acted as they did. And Blake. And Hobbes. You do not have to know, you merely have to think.

Religion, thought Hobbes, is not a safeguard against fear but a parasite on it. Prudence made him an Anglican, as I'm afraid it makes me, but he regarded all priests as cheats. Exiled to France, and believing himself near to death, he begged the clergy of three denominations to leave him alone, threatening, it is said, to 'detect all your cheats from Aaron to yourselves'.

So when I saw Pershore, I buckled at the knees. The remains of the abbey there, the transepts and tower, are so huge it is impossible to imagine the whole as it was. It struck me as oppressive, a cavernous yellow-stone yawn. Try as I might, I could not love it, or the men who made

129

it. I pitied them, and the poor people who now maintain it. I preferred Bredon's St Giles, with its readily detachable spire ('You take it down in sections,' said David Brown) and its note of companionship.

And I also preferred the church at Great Malvern. Who would not? It is uniformly fifteenth century, a true wool church, exuding pride, but love has not been driven out. It vaunteth itself, yes; but it has something to vaunt: those windows! And, like Bredon, it is uplifting.

But my favourite is Little Malvern Priory. Love really rests here. Its situation is unrivalled. You approach it and greet it as you would an old friend. Its tower is, much more than Pershore's, a lantern to your feet. You must, of course, walk up the hill where it nestles in old south-facing grounds, mellow and welcoming – bosomy, almost – but not tricked out; a real Rip Van Winkle place, just as it might have been left when the last of a dwindling band of monks fell asleep on the lawn and the grass grew over them. How small those monks were may be seen by a door inside. All the timbers are natural oak, grey and hard as stone; and the stone is natural limestone, than which there is nothing more beautiful on earth. The eloquent windows are light and high. The tiny doorways, blocked arches, peepholes and the carvings on the arm-rests of the monks' stalls (one of pigs feeding out of a pot) evince a proper sense of scale: the minuteness of man, and the majesty of God.

I felt this again at Deerhurst, that other sleeping beauty of the Malverns. Nothing can approach Tewkesbury's stout magnificence, but nearby Deerhurst is perhaps the ultimate revelation. Retiring into the fields, by a riverside farm, almost lost down a lane, it is light as the air that surrounds it. Alas, there are red-brick bungalows between it and the older Saxon chapel down the lane. It is as if a wicked fairy godmother has been determined to break up the happy partnership, interposing herself in the form of a raspberry-coloured garden gnome.

I was to spend the next three days hopping out of one
fat Bishopric into another: out of the county and bosom
of Worcester into the county and bosom of Hereford, and
vice-versa. From see to see.

On a May morning on Malvern Hills, in a summer
season when soft was the sun, I, like William Langland,
rested on a broad bank by a bourne and was lulled into
a dream; I was looking down to Severn plain, to

> *A faire felde fyl of folke. . .*
> *Of alle manner of men, the mene and the riche,*
> *Worching and wandryng as the worlde asketh.*

I spent an evening there too, which perhaps accounts for
the confusion and duality of my view. For you can stand
at any point on those hills when the air is clear and imagine
that you can see the whole world, as it was in the beginning,
is now and – God willing – ever shall be. It really is the
place to have a vision of time and space unlimited. (Think
of Vaughan, Herbert and Traherne who were all affected
by those views.) History is brought into proportion, past
and present merge; Langland is modern, today's headlines
are not. The horizon holds promise of no better world than
this.

I had just been reading an essay on Thomas Hobbes.
Like Langland, Hobbes was a great revolutionary. Like
Ruskin and so many other great Englishmen, he was also
a lover of mountains and the Derbyshire peak district was
his youthful stamping ground. Late in a life of discourse,
travel and study, he concluded that all knowledge is due
to sensation, and that the life of man in a state of nature

is 'solitary, poore, nasty, brutish and short'. Turning his back on books, he now gave himself entirely to thought: pure, logical thought. The result – *Leviathan* – is the book by which he is remembered still today.

Hobbes' principal axiom is that man is driven by fear. Fear of the dark. We all know what that means in a child; but, with the acquisition of a thick skin of experience, the adult covers it up.

Man, Hobbes believed, sought an answer from the Church which, in turn, exploited his fear, particularly 'the fear of darkness and ghosts, which is greater than other fears'. Hobbes and hobgoblins coloured my mind.

No hobgoblin or foul fiend troubles Colwall, where the church, the farm (once the Bishop of Hereford's hunting lodge) and the ancient alehouse remain intact and aloof. To say they are detached from the rest of the village is an understatement: they are a Sabbath day's journey away.

I was happy to see at Mathon a field full of folk – and that field, the churchyard! It was Rogation Sunday. The vicar and his folk had been beating the bounds of the parish and blessing the crops. He was just billowing back, his surplice a foaming wash in his wake, like a ship returning to dock. The lych-gate was a tight constraint. Camera at the ready to capture this summery scene, I squeezed through the cow-parsley, head-high and triumphing over the wall, and a full-blown Nevada rose. I was positioned well enough to see and not be seen. A man in his shirt sleeves was ready to play the violin. It was a sight that Hardy would have been loth to miss: a sight as old – and modern – as the cow-parsley. And the sound? The sound was as ancient – and modern – as bees settling on the honeysuckle and singing – or rather droning – 'For the beauty of the earth. . . .' There were women and children in bright summer frocks with here and there a wide-brimmed hat. Perhaps it was the churchwardens who were formally dressed, their 'wands' reminding them of their grave responsibilities. There were one or two panama hats; a rose buttonhole, too. But the men generally were at ease: a sight not often seen outside a pub. The sun winked on the clips of their braces and beamed on some bald heads. There is a tie that binds in a graveyard.

'Grant that they who have loved and served you here and are now at rest. . . .' The vicar's dignified intoning of the final prayer for the faithful departed set the seal on this perennial communion with earth, one which I fain would have joined earlier, but which I now realized I could only leave in peace.

I was staying in Hereford, my favourite of the smaller cathedral cities, with a favourite friend. Small though she is, she has the energy of ten – and needs it. She feeds the cathedral staff.

She had the Bishop's dinner to prepare and serve that week, so we agreed to keep out of each other's way. I paid my respects to the cathedral, saw how much money was needed (was it hundreds of pounds a second, a minute, a day?), bought a couple of apples at a greengrocer's and drove out of town. I wanted to see more of Hereford and Worcester's smaller, less expensive shrines.

I found myself on the Bromyard road. (Traffic round Hereford spins like a Catherine wheel: not the harmless firework, but the original devised for torture, with knives and teeth turning different ways.) Ocle Pychard, Much Cowarne, Stoke Lacey, lay ahead; and, beyond Bromyard, Bredenbury, Edwyn Ralph, Edvin Loach, Stoke Bliss. . . . Then the valley of the Teme. I should see Cradley, Bosbury, Clifton and Stockton; and, before I had finished, Aconbury, Kilpeck and Kilvert's Clyro perhaps. Oh, happy traveller I! *Bon appétit!*

In Bromyard I stopped to post a letter. First I had to buy an envelope. I found a shop with packets of fifty.

'I've got stamps, too,' said the shopkeeper, helpfully. I was so pleased not to have to spend time finding the post office, I put the stamp on and, pen in hand, waltzed out. Oh, the perils of waltzing! I was quite carried away. And so was my letter. Secure in that street pillar box was an envelope, virgin white, stamped, sealed, with my letter inside – but no address. I had the presence of mind to notice that the first collection had been made, and that the next would be at 12.15. I had time to go to Stoke Bliss.

At Stoke Bliss I was struck by the closeness of the church and farm expressed in a notice issued by the Citizens Advice Bureau and displayed in the church porch: FARMING COMMUNITY FACES MANY PROBLEMS. THE C.A.B. OFFERS FREE, CONFIDENTIAL SUPPORT AND ADVICE. Inside the church were displayed plans for its improvement and repair:

- Bird proofing of belfry-tower and spire
- Repair of fractured purlin and replacement of ridge tiles
- Repair and draught-proofing of South door
- Organ full of bat droppings
- Pews have anobium punctatum etc.

From the tower came the delighted squawk of a jackdaw at feeding time, followed by a shrill chorus of nestlings, followed by contented silence – for a while.

At the farm I saw my first shorn sheep, and blossoms of wild rose. It was terrible to think that, when all nature appeared at its prime, the worm, the canker, the gall-mite were at work.

It was noon when I parked my car for the second time that day in a Bromyard side street and planned how best to intercept the Royal Mail. A café stood nearly opposite the pillar box. I would lie in wait there. Coffee and apfelstrudel appealed, so mouth and mind worked as I kept watch for the postman's red van. Savouring my apfelstrudel, which was better than any I had tasted in Vienna, I must have momentarily lost concentration. The postman's van was already parked in a side street, and he returning to it dangling a pregnant bag. It was premature, this collection, I thought. Mouth covered in crumbs, I hasted out.

'Your Honour,' I nearly spluttered – he being an officer – 'Er, please. . . .'

I explained my anxiety. Important information. . . . Not just an ordinary letter.

'I understand,' the postman said. He whiffled with his hand inside the bag, May 19th's noonday sun lighting on secrets never-to-be-told. There was at least one letter in that bag without a stamp.

'Oh, mine's got a stamp,' I said. 'First class. But no address – can you believe it?'

The postman, sandy-haired, smiled. 'It's not near the top.'

'The last shall be first . . .' went through my head. 'I only posted it a short time ago,' I said aloud. 'If you turned the bundle over when you picked it up, it may be – there it is!' He lifted it out, my letter, as if it were an errant child, and delivered it into my hand to correct.

'I always wait a few minutes,' he said. And in what remained of those few minutes he gave me the history of Bromyard, centred on its eleven pubs.

'It is,' he said, 'a friendly town.'

That done, I motored out to Edwyn Ralph in the District of Gedeven. In Norman times, the church guide says, it belonged to Osbern Fitzrichard whose lands fell to the Ralfs and the de Loges, rival families who inspired Doone-like legends in these parts. From hillside fastnesses on either side of a valley, when not actually fighting, they appear to have tried to starve each other out.

One of the legends is of two knights who fought with swords for the same lady's hand. She rushed between them to break up the fight, was cut through – from either side – and they were so furious they fought till they died.

Lying in the west end of that church is a whole congregation of figures in stone, surpassing, the guidebook says, any of the kind elsewhere.

Outside, the sun shone on the trim churchyard. A man in short sleeves with both forearms heavily bandaged, his face badly grazed and looking as if he had been in a fight, was tending – he said – his mother-in-law's grave. I asked him where the village was. He seemed surprised, checked with the sun, and pointed to Bromyard 'over there'.

Edwyn (or Edvin) Ralph (or Ralf) is just a church in the fields. There is not even a farmhouse near by. But it won an award last year for the best-kept graveyard in Herefordshire – thanks, I suppose, to some who still fight.

At Aconbury, to the south of Hereford, the fight was on, too. Such was the triumph of cow-parsley at the bottom of the lane where I left my car that I could hardly see the farm and the church at the top, or the lone pine dwarfing the little belfry and spire, or the herd of Friesian cows skittishly blowing and showing off, freshly loosed that morning into the field. They seemed to have thrown off all care. What might have been dames were now girls. They kicked up their heels and, metaphorically, threw up their skirts in a cancan. They reminded me of a company of nuns I once observed bathing in the sea below Ardmore in Ireland, whooping and sploshing about fully clothed. It would be wrong to say I surprised them. They surprised me.

These cows were similarly wrapped up in themselves and their morning affairs. They were beating the bounds of this field – a fresh heaven of grass. Blow you! One pushed her face through the fence and gave me 'the eye'. Two set up a fight at the top of the hill, pawing the ground and butting it with their heads, like bulls. Support arrived quickly. Sand was flying. Heat and dust. Those pure pedigree black and white nuns were smirched with red dye. They had discovered a spring!

The road led me round to the church and the farm. Two collies slid in and out, as if in charge of both. It occurred to me that this may be the reason why Hereford churches are seldom, if ever, locked: a symbiosis of body and soul. Freedom was certainly in the air here, on top of a hill, on a May morning early.

Shocks were in the air, too. Audible snorts still came from the field. Time and the wind had dealt blows to the church. One of the struts of the old oak porch was lying across the floor. A list was drawn up on the door: PLANS FOR ACTION BY THE CHURCHYARD CONSERVATION GROUP.

1. Prepare for walkway
2. Bury rubble
3. Dig up brambles
4. Tidy up graves
5. Secure falling stones

The dogs still slid in and out as I left. The cows had settled down. Aconbury, I later discovered, was once a nunnery.

I was heading for Kilvert's Bredwardine. This, like all Herefordshire villages after ten o'clock on a weekday, was deserted, its commuters all moved out. An elderly man was mowing his roadside strip of lawn. I slowed to catch his eye, but could not catch his ear, his motor-mower making more noise than strike aircraft overhead. Just then I glimpsed the sign to the church and turned into the lane. A glide up a hill, bosky with may, horse-chestnut, box and yew, brought me to where the diarist lies. What matters it now, I thought, that he would see, in 1992, no women in bonnets sunning themselves by cottage doors, no Gipsy Lizzies in the lane, no boys bird's nesting, no Hereford cattle on the meadow by the Wye?

The path led round by the stuccoed Court: rambling and pretentious, Italianate with arches and colonnades, leading to apparent emptiness. The blinds were drawn. The maids have gone.

The walls of the church lean outwards, as if the silence is a strain. Tucked away under his memorial – a slab of stone like a table on four short legs – Kilvert's body lies; but his spirit, you imagine, is back in Clyro where he was happiest in his busy curate days, where I was hastening now.

On the way, I stopped in Hay where I found only books: second-hand, antiquarian, 'recycled' books. To find a Richard Jefferies was like looking for a needle in a haystack. Amaryllis was not at the fair. Jefferies, though prolific, was very collectable, I was told. He was not to be come upon in these Haystacks of books.

At Clyro I parked my car in the shade. Concentrating on this, and studying a small elderly man approaching on foot, I asked: 'Do you know where Parson Kilvert lived?'

'Right there,' he said, pointing to the tall grey house at my back, wisteria-clad. A plaque confirmed the fact.

'You a fan?' he asked.

'Yes,' I replied. 'Are you?'

'No – the locals here generally aren't.'

I talked of other things: the heat, the drought, the low level of the river, the Baskervilles. He opened up. He told me that the cottages in the village had mostly been bought by outsiders – they were too dear for the local people to buy. He pointed to a row of houses ahead, each one of which was sold for £140 in 1950; and a group of three, now knocked into one, which cost little more. Now they were worth £100,000 each at least. (I love the way a Welshman says 'at least'; he draws it from his mouth like a long sweet string of liquorice.) The Baskerville Arms, the black and white inn which stands opposite Kilvert's old lodgings, went for £3400 in 1950. A smallholding, inherited by his wife, rose in value he said, from £340 to £30,000 in their time together. She died some years ago of leukemia, contracted, he thought, while working on aircraft in the war – as others from the village had.

How old was he, my little man? He was clean and fair-skinned, clear blue-eyed, and had probably been ginger-haired when young. He had offered himself for employment as a twelve-year-old at Hay hiring fair for summer work on a farm at nine shillings a week. Later he got eighteen shillings on the Baskerville Estate. It was a traditionally low wage area, he said. He did not grieve for the Baskervilles' passing. He was, I thought, a well-preserved, gently-spoken piece of social history. Kilvert would have

139

loved him. I parted from him reluctantly.

But glad I did, for, on entering the church which was my main concern, I found a little man with broken teeth talking authoritatively to a lady from the States.

'And did the Reverend Kilvert deliver his sermons from that pulpit over there? Was it the very same one?' she asked.

'Well, it might not be the same,' he said. 'The church has been altered a lot.'

'I see,' she slowly swallowed the disagreeable fact. 'But how did such a small community fill such a lawge church?' she asked. 'Or perhaps it nay—vah did?'

'The Squire whipped them in,' I volunteered.

Her eyes lit up at this.

'Just like the churches back in the States where the Judge, the schoolteacher, and all in authority had to be present, regawdless of their belief – they had to be seen at the service.' Her speech only slightly quickened up.

'And what part of the States do you come from?' I asked.

'The Sow—wth.'

'The South's a big place.'

'Jaw—gee—ah'

'That's big, too.'

'Atlah—an—ta.'

She was a honey. Pleasure was packed into her little round body. She clutched a paperback copy of the Diary to her quivering breast. Her large glasses glinted. Her speech was like molasses.

'We speak real slow down there. . .'

The little man, whom I took to be the verger, gave us an authoritative review of the church and its heavy Victorian restoration, redecoration and extension – much of it done since Kilvert's time. He thought he recognized the artist in the stained glass style of one of the windows, but he failed to spot his wheatsheaf sign. The tower had once had a saddleback top. . . .

Something about this little man (how many of my chance meetings were with little folk!) prompted me to ask him if he were local.

'No,' he said. 'I come from Torquay.' He told us all about the caves there, the tiger and rhinoceros bones. . . . As a young man he had been a server in Exeter and had gone cycling, like Betjeman, to churches around – mostly wool churches, fifteenth century or later. So he liked the little old Herefords. There was passion as well as scholarship in his heart and head.

Back at the car, I studied the notice on Kilvert's house. I thought it said £100 to go in, returnable if you purchased something over £2000. (It was, of course, £1.00 and £20.00.)

Like a good fairy, the lady from Atlanta reappeared.

'It's just a picture gallery now,' she said; 'modern, avaunt gawd, you know. It's not officially open today, but the lady allowed me to see his room. There's nothing there – just a table to show where he wrote.'

She clutched the Diary ever more tightly as she stood there waiting, she said, for a taxi to take her back to Hay. Better pictures in that, I thought; imperishable, more precious than rubies – and priceless, because they are free.

'And where do you go on to from here?' she asked.

'Leominster and Shrewsbury,' I said.

'Lovely names!'

She loved my accent, she said.

Before going on to Shrewsbury from Leominster, I hopped back into Worcestershire. I had been invited to a Sheep Demonstration at Stockton on Teme. I was going to feast my eyes on a farm.

A few miles out of Hay, I called at a toll bridge over the Wye and asked the lady attendant if I might take some photographs. Between mouthfuls of what she explained was her lunch, she said yes. Permission granted, I photographed the river from a high point on the bridge and, back by the toll house, the charges board and description on either side of the window, making a triptych in black and white. What history, what ticks and tocks and springs and balance wheels have gone with Time's old rumbling cart across that bridge!

At Clifton church I called to see how James Strickland (aged seventy-two) was faring now: his tomb outside is taking off. It rears ready, as it were, for the Resurrection Trump. I wanted also to read again the Borough Charter in the porch, granted by Henry III in 1270, the 11th of May:

To the Archbishops etc., greeting. Know that we have granted and by this our charter have confirmed to Roger son of Roger de Mortimer that his town of Cliftone in the City of Worcester be a free borough for ever. . . .

What confidence that inspires! What pride, even today.

I wanted to see again the tomb of the thirteenth-century Knight with his faithful dog at his feet, and the memorial to Edward Jeffreyes, died 1725, 'Eminent in the law, Beloved by all that knew Him and adored by such as He Honoured with His Friendship.' His life must at least have overlapped that of his near namesake, George Jeffreys, the hanging judge.

My mind went back to my walk two years before, to that night in March when I stumbled down the hill-climb to Shelsley Walsh, through Stanford Bridge to 92 Worcester Road, Stockton on Teme.

*The sun had set behind yon hill, across the dreary
  moor. . .*
*When, weary and lame, a boy there came, up to the
  farmer's door. . .*

This afternoon, in contrast, the sun was high and my
spirits were excellent. As I swung down to the valley of the
Teme – surely one of the richest farming areas in Britain – I
felt full of pride for the beauty of my country, natural and
man-made. Here, where no road runs straight, the views
are breathtaking, of timeless, changeful hedgerows heaped
with may, bluebells, bursts of broom, waves of wine-leaved
sycamore, crowned red and white horse-chestnuts, lambs
on a hillock, and huddles of shade-seeking sheep.

The church above Stanford, set among cedars, looked
like a church in Tuscany. And, the church at Great Witley,
described as 'a Venetian Settocento Chapel in the English
Countryside', almost persuaded me I was in Italy.

When I finally parked my car at 92 Worcester Road,
I was glad to see that I was not. Here was what I had
long been searching for: the farm by the church – and a
fair field full of folk.

They had arrived by the charabanc load, from all over
England and Wales. Members of the Suffolk Sheep Society.
Bill, the high-priest, wore his panama hat. I offered to take
photographs. Go where you like, he said. Range free. That
was what I hoped he would say. I shot the ladies in the
sheds, sitting, sipping tea. I shot the ram worth twenty
thousand pounds. ('He could be dead in the mornin',' Bill
realistically remarked.)

There were sheep everywhere, cordoned, sectioned off;
groups of perhaps fifty or a hundred here, a group of sev-
en there. The luckier ones found shade under the orchard
apple trees, or tucked up by the churchyard wall.

143

The rams impressed me most. Some looked like aldermen, bishops even – conscious of their high calling, no doubt.

Keen-eyed men with crooks and thumbsticks stood respectfully admiring them. Their stillness showed that they had been admired before. There is a nonchalance about a Suffolk scion's Roman nose, a dusky dauntlessness about his eye, a stout affirmativeness in his feet, his solid stance, his 'topped off' level back, his generous endowment at the rear.

A border collie panted and patrolled, but proved redundant in this well-behaved society. A lilt of Welsh alighted in my ear: Da iawn – eez verry good! Duw, duw! Pink-eared, blue-eyed, with ageless sandy hair, the *Cymro* smiled a beatific smile. An elder of the chapel probably at home, there was no note of covetousness in his voice – only joy. Like everyone here, he was dressed for a good day out: collar and tie and polished boots. Like-minded shepherds and pedigree sheep, all well turned out, in a bond of respectful quietude.

A group of blond-headed Charolais steers stood stock-still in a covered yard. Bill's butter-mountain, I call them. Cutlery tinkled temptingly where ladies were serving teas in a covered yard beyond. I abstained and left instead to photograph the church.

A girl knelt back in the long grass of the graveyard painting the fourteenth-century porch. She had created a wonderful summery effect; colours swimming luminously, as if seen under water. We discussed the problems of photographing even a small church like this. If you get the height, you cannot get the width. . . I settled for a view of the porch, but from a wide angle that included something that – more than the nave and the heavily rebuilt chancel end, with its stubby belfry – caught my eye: the holly tree beside the path, with berries as red as any blood and blossom as white as the lily flower. Where had I seen that before? At Chedworth, two years, two months and many miles ago.

It was time for me to leave for Ludlow, where I was due at another farm. Returning to the car, I fancied that the same men were still in the same happy bond with their sheep, still making the same economical movements of trained hand and eye. It was a scene – apart from the coaches and cars – that their grandfathers would have recognized – and their grandfathers before them.

In one pen of seven superior tups, an elder was pointing – with that slow sure wave of a stick that shepherds and diviners have adopted over the years – to the one he thought was the best. Accompanying him in this selection test was a younger man bearing his toddler son on his arm. What would be the value of their collective wisdom and experience, I wondered? As much as that of the sheep? I thought I had struck a balance there.

Time seemed to have stood still that day. Spring was at its apogee. A herd of pedigree Friesian cows at Bayton lay like painted figures on a green hilltop. Untroubled as yet by flies, they were following the pattern of cows through the ages: travelling uphill with the heat, grazing on the way, then resting to chew the cud under trees obligingly placed there by enlightened farmers in the past. At milking time they would sway downhill like ships to port, bearing their fifty-pound cargoes of milk. One moves, they all move. Sensible moos!

I had three appointments to keep: one with Piers, one with Graham and one with Tom.

Piers was easy to find. His spirit resides in Cleobury Mortimer. In that temple of light, St Mary the Virgin's

Church.

The whole town of Cleobury lies on the tilt. The church is tilted; the street is tilted; the houses, shops and pubs are tilted; the people walk in a tilted way. It is a place to get an odd angle on things.

I stood with my back to the King's Arms, facing the church and trying to photograph the spire. The sky was Neapolitan blue, with windblown caravel clouds. The spire was cow-dung green – the flaking shingles had been weathered to the fibrous consistency of old thatch. An obtrusive board appealed for funds. A boy and a girl, hand in hand, took the dog for a walk, as thousands of couples had done before. They disappeared under the yews. Then Piers came into view: a boy who could have been of any age, curly-haired, casually – timelessly – dressed; a country lad come up to town. He stood up on the path which runs above the road in front of the church. A boy on a BMX bike rode up, spun, reared and disappeared. Piers stood his ground. Two high-school girls approached, chatting and licking ice-creams. I saw the thought pass through Piers' head. My chance! His tongue was quick to curl and claim a lick. The girl, the prettier of the two, advanced and then withdrew her hand. She smiled, passed on, without a second glance. The boy crossed over to the pub. 'Open all day,' it said. Quirky, his mind out of kilter with the times, young Langland would have done the same, I am sure.

More timeless pleasures lay ahead. I had been to the bookshop and picked up a good copy of Jefferies' last essays *Field and Hedgerow* and an early Penguin *The English Middle Classes* by Roy Lewis and Angus Maude. The latter I devoured. The former I delighted only in handling. I intended it as a gift for Graham, at whose home I was now due for tea.

Graham's other name is Bach. I first met him three years before when he was nearly twenty-one, a successful

146

Young Farmer who was in the news as an award winner at the Smithfield Show. I had called at The Rock, his father's farm near Ludlow, where he had shown me hundreds of beef cattle, cossetted in deep-litter barns. For all his youth he was a high quality judge of good stock: I could tell by the way he eyed and handled them. 'See that one with the mean head? That was one of my mistakes, but he'll kill out all right.' Graham's father had such confidence in him that he had already handed over most of the buying to him. I asked him how he did it, buying in lots not individually and competing against older heads with or without electronic calculators, and sharp, tongue-twisting auctioneers. He gained time, he said, by looking at the eye first, then running one hand down the flank; that way, he could tell all he wanted to know – while the others were 'messing about'. By the time they were tapping on their calculators, Graham had done his sums in his head. The vital thing was how the beast would grow on and how he would kill out.

Now Graham is not carnivorous. He is a gentle, quiet-spoken product of Shrewsbury School. He just happens to be no common marketeer. Above all, he is proud of his animals and looks after them well.

On this springtime visit I saw them all turned out in the fields, and it was my pleasure to go with Graham, after what he said had been a rough time for beef farmers, to see them coming into condition on grass such as he, in his young life, must rarely have seen.

'There's a good steer – the one with the Hereford face!' I was glad to see those Hereford-Friesian crosses coming back, with their characteristic bowed horns curving down. Dehorning became common practice with the increase in numbers of cattle kept in a confined space and, no doubt, with the introduction of more and more polled breeds lacking this natural means of defence. Sharp, upturned horns are dangerous and can be used to hike another beast almost to the point of puncturing the belly wall. But for these moon-faced, unassertive steers – as well-built as Rugby prop-forwards, but as docile as eunuchs in a harem or capons in a hen run – dehorning seems unnecessary, unnatural, painful and expensive.

'Happiness is a horned Hereford!' I exclaimed – and Graham, who studies the psychology as well as the physiology of his animals, agreed.

'Horns are by no means a detraction from the look of a beast, especially on open pasture like this,' he considered, quietly – his thinking as measured as his step.

The ground was level and well-drained on this table-land up on the Clee Hill road. 'We're as near organic as we can be,' said Graham, asking me if I minded climbing over the next gate. 'We have to put locks on our gates. People think they have a right to walk all over the fields and they don't always close gates. And. . .' I could see the worry pass over his brow '. . . that's why we keep dogs. Fortunately the house is not too near the road.'

My mind went back to a time when I was not quite Graham's age. At this time of year, we liked nothing better than walking in pasture like this, the time-honoured pleasure of looking round the ground. That meant running your hand down the flanks of a Hereford-cross-Shorthorn cow – with horns. 'Boy, she looks well!' It was a kind of fellowship, a communion extended to visiting friends. Those cattle were red and white or strawberry roan. They appeared to have dipped their heads in a bucket of whitewash and tossed it all over themselves.

I thanked Graham for reminding me of this; and, on parting, gave him the book. Would he read it, I wondered.

'Oh, he will,' said his father, 'and it won't take him long!'

I slipped back to Hereford that night, with thoughts of moving on to Ludlow next day. After forty years, I was going to see Tom.

Would he have become grey, fat, shambling and dull, that upright, bright, engaging youth whom I had admired but not known very well as a student, all those years ago?

I had been retired from teaching some seven or eight years already. Early retirement we called it; for me, however, it had not come a moment too soon. Tom, it appeared, had soldiered on.

It was quite by chance that I discovered his whereabouts, that he was still in the service, and had spent the last twenty years campaigning in this beautiful place. Seven was as much as I had managed at any one school. But that was Tom, and that was me.

It would be interesting to see how differently those forty years had dealt with us.


Ludlow had grown – spilled out, so to speak. I did not know where St Julian's Road was.

'If you want the road, it's the second on the right; if you want the avenue, it's the first.' With this information I guessed I was close.

A young man with a child in a pushchair put me right.

'Fernleigh? Mr Finney's? It's the one with the VW camper-van in the drive.' I guessed he had been taught by Mr Finney – and not all that long ago!

Tom came bouncing to the door in trainers, shorts, and a yellow T-shirt. He welcomed me in. He lived in a very big house. He had a full head of hair. Teaching had scarcely touched his dark-tan looks. He bounded upstairs.

'Come up,' he called. 'We live on four floors.'

Trumpety music greeted my ears. 'Handel?' I asked.

'Nearly,' said he.

'Purcell?'

'No, later than that.'

'Blind Stanley?' I was stumbling in the dark.

'William Boyce.'

I lowered my head into a mug of coffee while Tom turned the volume up.

He remembered me as languid, he said. I told him I had outgrown my strength.

After a tour of the house, which I could imagine Elgar living in, we went by camper-van to Ludford Bridge and the common beyond, where Tom pointed out views. He alluded to a poem he had written in 1976 when he and his two boys had walked on the islands in the river which formed when the water was low. He still wrote poetry – some published; for children mainly, light and amusing, he said. Teaching had not soured Tom, though we agreed that the good days were gone. He was enjoying his retirement, he said.

Back home, we talked of college days, our well-remembered tutors and friends. He had, in the attic, copies of our college magazines, *The Salt* and *Saltette*. He gave me two to read at home. And a copy of Housman's *Shropshire Lad* published by a local press, for which he had written the introduction. He could not, he said, have used the piece he had written as a student for *The Salt*. I understood why. The things we wrote then were good – but only for their time. We spiral upwards – or downwards – in life. The viewpoint shifts. We only think we have not changed.

We ate a healthy lunch, then did the next most healthy thing: we went for a long walk by the river to parts of Ludlow, Tom said, most of its inhabitants never reached. We circled the water meadows, 'hedges heaped with may', to where the Corve and Teme meet.

'There are views of the castle from here that others

never see,' said Tom, then launched into a recital of *A Shropshire Lad* which had stayed in his memory since he was seventeen. It would have been corny, had it not been so apt.

We parted with an exchange of books: islands in the river of time.

# In Ludlow Town

The castle itself is in the very perfection of decay. All the five courts, the royal apartments, halls, and rooms of state lie open, abandoned and some of them falling down, for since the Courts of the President and Marches are taken away, there is nothing to do that requires the attendance of any public people. So time, that great devourer of the works of man, begins to eat into the stone walls, and to spread the face of royal ruins upon the whole fabric.

Thus wrote the masterly Defoe in 1723, when the rest of Ludlow was at its Georgian apogee.

You can better perceive how splendid it might have been by popping into College Street, concealed from 'public people' who mostly throng the market place or quietly dribble into church but miss this slice of history wedged between.

There stand the Hosyers Almshouses, splendidly restored in Georgian brick with, in the main gable, a red lion couchant on a blue and white ground and gilded Latin inscription which, for twentieth-century and New Age travellers is translated below:

Hosyers Almshouses originally built by the munificence of John Hosyer, merchant, in the year of Salvation 1486, and through the damage of time weakened for a while and about to collapse, rebuilt 1758 in the reign of His Most August Majesty George II by the bailiffs, burgesses and community of this town of Ludlow.

One dignified elder descended the steps. I was tempted to ask him how he fared, but was afraid of receiving a Georgian rebuff. I slipped away to see how time was devouring the castle instead.

There, ticket booths and loudspeakers bespoke the approaching Festival. There was a party of schoolchildren with clipboards and a questionnaire. Rosalind was seated distantly on stage, her long dark hair hanging down to her waist. Was she learning her lines? No, doing something with her half-concealed hands. She might have been spinning with a drop spool, or practising her needlepoint. I watched from the bailey while stage-hands trafficked to and fro. They were mostly working on the same small apron of rock covered with green matting, surmounted by the crumbling walls, cluttered with the boughs of a very representational Forest of Arden. There was a wheel barrow on stage. There was also a large cardboard box.

'I know you have a thousand and one things to think about . . .' said a young producer's assistant to a man laying electrical cables along a gully in the sward. Emboldened by their engrossed states of mind, I peeped back-stage. There were trellises hung with golden apples, a copper firescreen which would serve as the Duke's scutcheon and still more lengths of wire and hooded lights. A burst from the tannoy announced that the public address system was under trial. 'One, two, three, testing . . . this is the Festival sound . . .' came the lady's breathless, excited voice.

Rosalind still sat by her box, quietly repeating her hand movements, but not apparently moving her lips. The men were mostly technicians, so they had nothing to say – only a thousand and one things to think about. Children ascended and descended the tower by the gate. One had dropped his clipboard and questions on the ground.

'How would you describe the ice house?' Answer: cold and small.

'Was there ever any water in the moat?' No, because it was a dry moat.

'What was the garderobe for?' Toilets.

'Why did Roger de Lacey build his castle here?' Good view and near a river for drowning. Drowning? My attention seemed to be wandering.

An indifferent youth, wired to a walkman and not attached to the school, passed wearing a T-shirt with the words FREEDOM & EASY EXPRESSION blazoned front and back. He looked a very mild sort of revolutionary to me.

Rosalind still sat, head down over her work, her own – or Shakespeare's – music going on in her head. I could now see what she was doing, and what was in the large box. She was threading apples on a string.

It would be easy to be contentious about Ludlow. It exudes civic pride, and has plenty to be proud about. Unforgettable among the many plaques set up on buildings by the town's Civic Society is the one outside 29 Broad Street: BIRTHPLACE AND BOYHOOD HOME OF JAMES VASHON 1742–1828 WHO JOINED THE NAVY AS A MIDSHIP-MAN AND ROSE TO BECOME AN ADMIRAL OF THE WHITE. I bow to James whenever I pass his house.

These plaques are a great help to the visitor. They tell you, for instance, that the Broad Gate itself is the only survivor of seven main gateways and that it is still in proud possession of its thirteenth-century drum towers and portcullis arch. They tell you also that 18 Broad Street was built as a town house for the Salweys of Richards Castle, prominent Parliamentarians and Whigs; and that Dinham House was the eighteenth-century town house used by the Knights of Downton, the Johnes of Croft Castle and the Earls of Powis, and that Napoleon's cousin Lucien Bonaparte was imprisoned here in 1811.

Everybody who was anybody came willingly or unwillingly to Ludlow in the past – or so it seems. I return willingly as often as I can, but I doubt if I shall ever manage a house.

155

The great distinction of Ludlow in the past – like that of other small towns of the marches – was topographical: its high position above and differentiation from the countryside around. It was, after all, the greatest – and remains the best preserved – of all the border castles, a royal stronghold, visited by Richard III and Henry VI and with a strong claim to have held out longest for Charles I in the Civil War. (Donnington Castle, near my present home in Berkshire, may have done better.)

But what draws me to Ludlow is the suspicion that its greatest benefactors were its new rich merchants who cocked a snook at the king. It is here that the mercers and landowners trumpeted their Parliamentarian and Whig convictions and preached – and practised – Civic Pride. It is here, perhaps, that England's heart beat most audibly and sensibly to the left.

Ludlow was still an important town when Milton wrote *Comus*, 'A Masque presented at Ludlow Castle, 1634, before John, Earl of Bridgewater, then President of Wales'.

He had, apparently, heard the story of the Earl's young daughter, the lovely Lady Alice Egerton, being lost in a ravine when out riding with her two brothers in Heywood Forest. The masque was presented in the hall of the castle on the anniversary of the adventure and Lady Alice took part in it, playing herself. An old life of Milton refers to her marriage, when she was much older, to the Earl of Carberry, Lord President of the Marches, whose official residence was Ludlow Castle. 'Thus,' it says, 'by a romantic chance, Lady Alice, now the Countess of Carberry, re-entered Ludlow Castle and graced once more, as mistress of it, the very hall in which 26 years before she had acted and sung in Comus.'

Now the great joy for me in re-reading *Comus* is to see, not only how beautiful the poetry is, but also how subtly Milton addresses his task. He sets the piece in 'a

wild wood'. Comus, the young lady's abductor, is really
a monster representing that most anathema of all things to
Ludlovians: Arbitrary Power. He enters 'with a charming-
rod in one hand, his glass in the other; with him a rout
of monsters, headed by sundry sorts of wild beasts, but
otherwise like men and women . . . they come in making
a riotous and unruly noise. . . .' But Milton immediately
gives to Comus these most beautiful, beguiling lines:

> *The star that bids the shepherd fold*
> *Now the top of heaven doth hold,*
> *And the gilded car of day*
> *His glowing axle doth allay*
> *In the steep Atlantic stream,*
> *And the slope sun his upward beam*
> *Shoots across the dusky pole,*
> *Pacing toward the other goal*
> *Of his chamber in the East.*
> *Meanwhile welcome joy, and feast,*
> *Midnight shout, and revelry,*
> *Tipsy dance, and jollity.*

Why, one asks, do Shakespeare at Ludlow, when one
could do this?

Milton uses the topography so well, seeing civic pride
as local pride writ large. Always strong on shepherds and
sheep, he brings help to the victim's anxious brothers in
the form of the Attendant Spirit who turns out to be
Thyrsis, their father's shepherd. He leads them to 'the
navel of this hideous wood' where Comus 'skilled in his
mother's witcheries' dwells.

The scene changes to a stately palace occupied by
Comus and his rabble, and the Lady set in an enchanted
chair, to whom he offers his glass, which she puts by. . . .

157

The brothers rush in with swords drawn, wrest the glass out of his hand, but fail to overpower him. The Spirit, entering, says:

> 'What, have you let the false enchanter scape?
> O ye mistook, ye should have snatched his wand.'

All is not lost, however. 'There is a gentle nymph,' the spirit says

> not far from hence,
> That with moist curb sways the smooth Severn stream,
> Sabrina is her name. . .

He then implores her powerful hand:

> 'Sabrina fair
> Listen where thou art sitting
> Under the glassy, cool, translucent wave,
> In twisted braids of lilies knitting
> The loose train of thy amber-dropping hair. . . .'

She responding, sprinkles on the Lady's breast 'drops from my fountain pure I have kept of precious cure. . .'

The trick is done. Everybody, including Sabrina, has good reason to haste away, 'the stars grow high, but night sits monarch in the mid sky.'

The final scene, presenting Ludlow town and the President's castle, is accompanied by country dancing and songs during which the children are presented by the Spirit to their father and mother. The dances ended, the Spirit delivers the epilogue.

Not to be outdone by the town, the Teme Valley villages from Downton to Pipe Aston were holding a festival that weekend. VISIT OUR VILLAGES, a notice said, FOR A TOUR OF THE CHURCH, TEAS WITH FLOWER DECORATION AND A WALK ROUND THE FARM. Irresistible, I thought, and – this being Thursday – arrived early at the feast.

The little Norman church at Pipe Aston sports a tympanum over the door. I went inside. It was not only open, it was inviting! A chair placed by the table in the open vestry opposite the main door, seemed to suggest that the Attendant Spirit, having just popped out, would be back anon; visitors, please feel at home.

Places like this immediately bring a smile to one's face. They are so companionable, these little Hereford churches – relatively unspoiled, uncluttered and at ease with themselves. They make you feel at ease, too.

Why, in all these churches that seem so welcoming, I wondered, do the walls lean out? These were pleasantly decorated with a flower pattern I had seen before somewhere: ah, Duntisbourne Rouse! The chancel was nicely distempered with cream. I think the Victorians were responsible for the flower pattern and probably the ladies doing the teas for the cream. At least there were no heavy memorials on the walls. I could not read the leaflet fixed behind glass which told about the tympanum *et al*, but it indicated that further information would be available at neighbouring Walley House.

I hied me on to Walley House, where I had earlier seen a man enter the drive on a tractor. I took it therefore to be a farm, and lunch time.

The house itself did not quite suggest a farm. There was a milk bottle by the door. I rang. A gentleman came. I told him my business. He asked me in.

'My brother would like to speak to you,' he said, taking me through to the living-room where the boiler-suited tractor operator was having his meal.

'Excuse me . . .' I repeated myself. 'I'm interested in the church, but I'm also interested in your cattle . . . a very good herd, I should think. . . .'

'Well, look in the window there!'

I was shown, in a passage, a glass case holding show awards, first prize cards and rosettes and pictures of a champion Charolais steer, the Lad.

'But whose are the Friesians I saw near the church?' I asked.

'Oh, they're not ours, they belong to the Elton Estate.'

I was given a cup of tea, a seat and – what is so common in villages, and among farmers especially – a smile to cover my *faux pas*. They quickly disregard your ignorance and put you at your ease.

The brothers gave me insights into what had happened to the other farm. It was part of the Elton estate, but the house had been sold off and planning permission sought to convert the barns. It is a common story nowadays. Money is tight and the developments do not continue apace as initially proposed.

Their own farm consisted partly of glebe land – up to fifty acres, they supposed; and their house was the old rectory. They had a spring in the field on the hill, so they would never be short of water, even in a dry summer.

'Is the church well supported?' I asked.

'Oh, yes, pretty well,' they said.

Luncheon over, my attention more happily directed to the Charolais herd. John, in his overalls and wellington boots led me out to the field where, in the manner of stock well looked after, the cows – and even the bull – came up and licked our hands. The bull liked to have one finger inserted in his ear.

'That's one spot they cannot reach themselves,' John said.

Seeking shade in one of the sheds was Lucky, his favourite cow. I murmured about the depth and buttery nature of her build, her kind eye and contented nature. She did stand out above the rest – but so she would have done in any company. Her daughter stood alongside her, buttery and good-natured too.

'What do you call her?' I asked.

'Oh, she's only got a number,' said John.

'Then, I'll have to give her a name,' I laughed.

It struck me as odd that, among all these cows which John had bred and reared intimately, knowing all their genetic inheritance and treating them all equally well, only one had a name.

John showed me a cow with two young calves indoors, and another young steer, Lucky's son, I believe, and full-brother of the Lad. It still seemed strange that this friendly, fatherly man knew his animals only by numbers, apart from Lucky and the Lad. He treated them all so affectionately, like children in fact. We talked about the deer I saw grazing on one of the fields high up near the woods which, everywhere here, clothe the hills.

'Do you mind them?' I asked.

'I like to see them,' he said. 'They're a unique variety of fallow deer – long-haired. They're found nowhere else in the world. I'm a member of the Deer Society,' he added, 'and we're pledged to keep them like that.'

Here was a man, I realized, who was in the mould of the great and good farmers like George Henderson, whose principal concern was care: care for the land and its continuing well-being, care also for the quality of the stock. 'The better the breed, the less the feed,' and, 'I'd rather keep one quality beast then ten poor beggars,' are the kind of dicta they shared. By good management and

161

low waste John could gladly support fellow-travellers like me and a few fallow deer.

By now, one happy cow was licking John's face.

'She likes to chew my chin,' he said. 'She's short-sighted, see.'

It was time for me to leave. We passed Lucky's shed again. She and her daughter were now lying down, contentedly chewing the cud, a picture of bliss.

Still worrying about her having no name and to register my pleasure at the hospitality I had received I made a bold suggestion to my host.

'I know what you should call the daughter,' I said.

'What?' said John.

'Happy,' I said.

Was Rosalind still threading apples on a string when I returned to town? I do not know. I decided to end my review of Ludlow at that fairly indestructible monument to Civic Pride, the parish church.

However askance one may look at the Victorian 'improvements' – the heavily restored stained-glass, the hefty but imposing superstructure of the oak choir stalls, the smooth refacing of the rough red sandstone in and out, you have to admire the whole effect. Milton would have felt at home here.

Here, among grand tombs of the Sydneys and Townshends, Lord Presidents and Chief Justices of the Council of the Marches of Wales, are such endearing memorials as these:

HEARE LYET SUSAN THE
WIFE OF JOHN RICARD
GENT TOWNE CLARK

IN LUDLOW TOWN

OF LVDLOW BY ADAM
IN THE DUST I LYE
BY CHRIST I AVE THE
VICTORY
1640

and

In Memory of Theophilus Sawley Esq<sup>re</sup>
who was the eldest son of Edward Salwey,
a younger son of Maj. Richard Salwey,
   who in the last Century
   sacrifiz'd all and everything in his Power
   in support of publick liberty
   and in opposition to Arbitrary Power.
Pro Rege Saepe Pro Republica Semper.

There also to remind Milton of his times is a notice in the
Lady Chapel telling how two hand-operated iron-wheeled
'Fire Engines' of 1669 were kept in the church with a very
small opening in the wall to allow passage of them and their
doughty attendants.

Only men who are good know what to do with liberty
– or something like that, Milton said.

'Fashinatin', ishn't it?' said the Attendant Spirit by
my side. 'Mushn't menna bin small in zhoges dayges?'

He was middle-aged, had been curly-haired, his hair was
now thinning and so were his teeth. He darted a keen-eyed
look at me. He was half-Puck, half-Touchstone, I thought
– and wholly Lob. He had dark eyes under bushy brows,
the sort that vigilantes need. You see them in the men of
Clun.

'Sheen the Mishericordes?' he said.

'Not yet,' I answered – affecting a certain hauteur.

'I'll zhow ya zem.' With one bound of his old-time
boots, he landed among the misericords – the carved
seats of the choirstalls which were supposed to be so

163

uncomfortable that their occupants could not fall asleep.

'Zsha hale-house wife's my fayverit,' he said. 'And zsha Pieta, on zsha enda zshat pew!' He pointed a hand barely showing from the sleeve of his outsized coat. 'Shee!'

'I would never have noticed that,' I said, peering with him at the tiny carving on the inside of the hand-rest of the first choir-stall. It was worn by many a soft precentor's hand, I thought. How different from the hand of the mediaeval carpenter who had carved it and put such passion into it, causing it to be admired by Lob and me – and many thousands like us over possibly five centuries.

'Poshably,' he agreed.

And then I lost him in the dark. I don't know where he went. Back to his own time, whenever that was.


I went out into the light and airy graveyard: the Garden of Rest, I think it's called, whence all the stones have been removed. I stood with my back thrust into the old door of the choir vestry and snapped the Reader's House. I tried to imagine a man in that office in the last century, pausing in his Jacobean doorway, with his Victorian high hat in one hand and his high sermon in the other. How hard it would have been for him to have thoughts of anything other than his own distinguished well-being! Perhaps it was he in whose memory friends restored the fifteenth-century window in the Chapel of St John the Evangelist near by: the Rev Robert Menricke BA, 50 years Reader of Ludlow, 1876.

He would have seen the graveyard with all its stones – or most of them – upright and intact. In about 1930 they were all bundled round the back of the church: the Davenports, the Beauchamps, the Grosvenors along with the Cooks. Better to be remembered like Richard Davies in the same Chapel 'who in the habitual Exercife of Piety,

Charity, Temperance, difcharged all the Duties of a private life and exchanged it for immortality 1739'. Or like Housman, whose stone stands next to a cherry tree in a secluded corner of the Garden of Rest.

> *Goodnight, ensured release*
> *Imperishable peace;*
> *Have these for yours.*

The first swaggery notes of Bach's D minor Toccata burst from the organ and shattered my dream. I did not see Lob again, any more than the Reader with his high hat, or the small bushy-browed men of 1669 busily wheeling their Fire Engines out.

# The End of the Rainbow

'*Mae haul yn gweni* – the sun is smiling!' This is Llanr-haeadr: a burst of Welsh greeting, obligingly translated.

I arrived early. It was Saturday. The little town was *en fête*. Ellen greeted me at Dolawel, her house backing onto the hill. Her collie, Fly, did a Bo-peep ballet on the small apron stage at the front of the house. I was accepted; I was given a paw, in exchange for a pat.

'You'll be going to the Pistyll?' said Ellen, after a cup of tea.

'Of course. And you?'

'I'll stay and make dinner. Then Liz will come and we'll take you to Briw. You'll like that?'

'Of course!'

How could anyone not like Lanrhaeadr? It is End-of-the-rainbow-land for me.

Ellen was born at Tan-y-Pistyll, the house which is now a café at the foot of the Pistyll – the waterfall. It is fully four miles from the town where she and her brother went to school. It is a steep ride down on a bike. Described as a single track road with passing places, it is also a steep drive up in a car. There are one or two smallholdings on the way. Sheep roam the roadside and the rocky, rushy fields. Occasionally they break through the fence. You stop your car by a gate to try to help an agitated, scatter-brained ewe, separated from her lamb. She runs on, doubles back, plunges into a grassy defile, pops up again. She is not beyond the point of no return, but you worry about her lamb – or lambs. You ought to tell the farmer. The Good Shepherd would be out of his wits with this ewe!

At the Pistyll itself the sheep seem more composed. Cars have been left in parking places fifty or a hundred

167

yards away. Two-legged man adopts a kind of crippled gait. He stands amazed. He feeds his face. He takes a measured stroll across the chasm by the little iron bridge. He is cut down to size.

I had never stopped long by the café before, preferring to range free, like the sheep on the hill. Now I noticed how tidy and well-preserved the old place was. Chalet-like, it was built of weathered stone with low-pitched roof and overhanging eaves. The pillared, veranda-type porch gave it the extra-welcoming look of a traditional mountain homestead that could be anywhere in the world. An old mangle, whose well-chewed wooden rollers had wrung many a wool blanket and shirt, stood idle by the door. A cheese press, solid iron, boasting of having been made by T. Corbett, Shrewsbury, and exhibited at London, Birmingham and Amsterdam, stood, as they say, hard by. My eye was caught by an athletic ewe rearing up like a deer to reach the leaves of a sycamore tree. A family of Germans who had earlier parked their VW camper-van by my car now posed before the waterfall, father filming them from the footbridge while I snapped him filming them. . . . The children wore bright anoraks: the nearest I would come today, I thought, to a rainbow in the spray.

It was an image, cherished from childhood, that 'rainbow in the spray': real or imaginary, seen or only heard of, I did not know.

'Did you ever see the rainbow in the spray?' I asked Ellen, over lunch.

'Oh yes,' she said, unsurprised. I was reassured, relieved. Then Liz, her daughter, arrived. She was full of enthusiasm for Briw.

'Where is Briw?' I asked.

'Near Priddbwll, you know!' I had been to Priddbwll Ganol, the farm where Liz and her brother Tudor were brought up. Impossible to pronounce or spell, it was another of those enchanting names given to enchanting places around Llanrhaeadr: Tai Bach, Cefn Coch, Penygarnedd, Penybontfawr. . .

'How do you spell Briw?' I asked.

'B – r – i – w! In Welsh we pronounce every letter, and every letter is always the same,' Liz patiently explained.

'I see,' I said. But Welsh is as unattainable to me as the rainbow – and just as attractive.

We drove to Briw by car, I protesting that I wanted to walk.

'You'll walk far enough,' said Liz, taking bend after bend uphill.

We passed by Priddbwll Ganol fields and a house tucked into the hill called Frwynen, which, Liz said, was her favourite, now and when she was a child.

We parked by a chapel.

'This is Briw,' Ellen said, with the pride that all Welsh people reserve for their Bethels in the hills. We met the lady who now lives at Priddbwll, our hostess in charge of the teas. And the man in charge of the walk. He wore a jacket and hat. Most other men, like me, were in short-sleeved shirts. Some walked with crooks, some with hazel thumb-sticks. There was a gathering of about a hundred now, called to order by the minister, I think, who introduced us to our guide, the man in jacket and hat, an elder of the church, a shepherd patriarch.

We advanced in orderly procession, by steep lanes lined with laburnum, he pointing out features of interest on the way: a derelict house here, a restored one there – part of the Wynstay Estate. The ladies were all in their summer clothes, mainly white. At the top of the hill, those of us in the lead were outpaced by eager photographers, some taking moving pictures of the 'flock' that stretched down-hill now, and on out of sight. All around us were hills, which the patriarch pointed out: Cil Mawr and Cil Bach –

169

Big Nook and Little Nook; Aran Fawr – Big Hill; Canol yr Aran – Middle Hill; the Gyrn – Peak. Everywhere there were sheep.

Emyr, my friend from Cefn-y-braich, assured me that it was a fact that forty per cent of all the sheep in Britain are to be found within a radius of sixty miles from Welshpool.

'That would include Ledbury,' I suggested.

'True,' he answered, making it nearly rhyme with Briw.

I asked him what he thought of the new CAP agreement on sheep.

'I have not seen all the details yet,' was his cautious reply. It went well with his measured step. You do not rush to conclusions on these hills. I was glad when he invited me for a *paned* (a cup of tea) at the farm and to see Carys, his wife.

I had forgotten, with all this ambling and easy conversation with friends, what was our purpose in gathering at Briw.

'To raise chapel funds. We're a dwindling congregation, you see,' the Patriarch confirmed.

Back at the chapel, we had tea with home-made cakes and sandwiches. There was an exhibition of old and new photographs, illustrating community life here over many years. There was a display of old tools and a range of old record books and a Directory of Wales, open at the point where the authors had written of Denbighshire: 'The air of this county is efteemed healthy, but it is rendered sharp and piercing by a vast chain of mountains which, for the much greater part of the year is covered by snow.'

'Amen,' I said.

The wind was tugging at my shirt as we sat outside to eat our tea. Ellen and Liz were in full agreement with my breaking ranks and going with Emyr to Cefn-y-braich. By back lanes and bumpy Land Rover we went. A *paned* and a farm kitchen chat set me up, my faith restored in education, the church, farming and youth, among other matters we discussed. Carys, already a headmistress, was doing a B. Ed. degree. Noel, their son, was growing into a fine, articulate lad. My only regret was that they were not coming to the dance. They were too busy, they said.

The dance! Billed as part of the current Festival of the Arts in Llanrhaeadr, this was to be the climax of my evening. It was advertised as Welsh Folk Dancing with Dawnswyr Delyn at 7.30 p.m. in the Village Hall.

Emyr delivered me back to what is known as the village, which I call the town. Ellen was there in the street. I dropped off. Just like that.

Liz had gone home: another one busy, putting her house up for sale. Ellen, retired like me, conceded a spot of dancing might be fun.


The village hall recalled for me old halls of childhood, made of tin and wood, bright with elbow-grease and improvisation, fragrant in summer with lilac and eau-de-Cologne, in winter with cigarette smoke and brilliantine, warm with the sun or 'slow-but-sure' old Tortoise stove.

Llanrhaeadr's had a bar. Beer flowed. The dancers, in costumes of red, green, mauve and gold were taking to the drink. They outnumbered – and outmanoeuvred – the audience! They, if not we, were gathering strength. Half-past seven became eight o'clock. Everyone, including a young couple – holiday-makers, I supposed – with their two small children, was very relaxed. It was a real village 'do'.

The dancing was excellent, when it began. The courtly dress suited the style of the dance. The audience was invited to join in. I found myself spinning down the lines of the set and forming an arch at the bottom with my lace-sleeved lady, graciously smiling, setting the pace. Even the young

171

man's two-year-old son joined in, proving that if you can toddle you can dance. In the more bravura passages he was borne on his father's arm, or spun by him, shoulder-high, down the line.

'*Eto* – again!' the little boy cried.

Twirl and spin, side-step and follow – it's easy, when you know how.

Somewhere in all this toing and froing I passed Ellen holding on to her beau.

'One more?' I suggested when we sat down.

'One more,' she sighed.

Swifts were skimming the tight slate roofs of the town when we threaded our way through the street back home. A thousand male voices from Cardiff burst out of the television screen. Rhosymedre, Myfannwy, Calon Lân. . . Denis O'Neil sang 'Nessun Dorma' at the top of his voice. The choirs, subdued, sang 'Steal Away'. I said to Ellen, '*Da iawn. Diolch yn fawr*. . . I'll steal away.' And did.

# Full Circle

One of the rooms in our old house at Little Ness was called the Empty Room. Another we called the Tunnel of Light.

The Empty Room was not empty at all. It was full of books, mostly belonging to my mother's side of the family, self-made people from Liverpool, freetraders and social reformers, much influenced by the wave of civic idealism engendered in the 1870s by Joseph Chamberlain. Birmingham, Manchester and Liverpool – *pace* Engels and Marx – were then rising centres of trade, bringing us wealth from our empire and new-found pride to the expanding middle classes, to which the Cowells belonged.

Bulking large on their bookshelves were Chamber's *Encyclopaedia*, Samuel Smiles' *Self-Help*, the works of Dickens, Ruskin and Charles Kingsley; and, slipped in between, *The Story of an African Farm*, *The Cigarette Maker's Romance*, *Handy Andy* and *Sybil, or The Two Nations*. Disraeli's father, Isaac, was represented there, too, with *Curiosities of Literature*. There were books of art and music. (It was there that I first learned about 'The Harmonious Blacksmith' and 'The Magic Flute'.) The *Origin of Species* was there, and those other great probings of the mind, Blake's *Poetry and Prose*, Locke *On Human Understanding*, John Stuart Mill *On Liberty* and Montaigne with his motto: Know Thyself.

Here, behind glass doors, were enshrined all my grandfather's and great-grandfather's expectations and ideals, their efforts to grasp and hold onto the benefits of this traffic of the mind as well as to pocket a few pounds in the process. They had extended themselves intellectually – though there was one black sheep uncle, and the male line had died out, leaving only Mother, our great-aunt Alice and us as beneficiaries. We may not have realized it at the time, but something of their spirit and vision must have entered our slow-waking minds through their books.

Sometimes *Unto This Last*, *Uncle Tom's Cabin*, Kingsley's *Heroes* or *Hereward the Wake* went up to bed with us, to that other oddly named room, christened by my brother the Tunnel Of Light: a long, low-ceilinged room with odd angles and beams.

There, by torch and candle-light, we wrestled with Theseus against the Minotaur, counted up to a million, traced the War of the Worlds and tracked the Time Machine. We cracked social codes, discovered illegitimacy, and I – if not he – became a little radical. I read *The Village Labourer* – which my grandfather would not have known. When I went to Saltley in 1949, I was an unbridled colt.

Now, in 1992, I was going back to that dark tunnel of grime. The prosperity of the 1980s had given us the new M40 linking with the M6 and the Black Country. A quick turn onto the A47 brought me to signs which said Birmingham E., Washwoodheath Road, Alum Rock and College Road. Past Kashmir Jewellers, Ibraham News, Jamil Fashions, signs saying PAY NO POLL TAX, familiar Hartopp Road and St Saviours Road, I came to: *Nulla Sine Sale Salus*, St Peter's College, Number 188 College Road. There were no sleepy-eyed students. The college, closed in 1978, is now some sort of educational trust. There was no Coutts Tobacconist, no coffee shop, no Morris Cowley works.

I parked in the College forecourt at a few minutes after eight. A man with a bunch of keys at his belt and a clutch of wine glasses in his hand smiled as he went on his busy way.

'You're looking after us?' I said, with an old campaigner's confidence.

'I'm doing my best,' he said.

Only the little bob-hole, like a door into a hutch, had been open when I drove into the forecourt and parked my car. Now the whole great double door was thrown aside. Two men in grey suits advanced.

'I'm Jack Butcher,' said one. I told him who I was, and struggled to frame my next remark. Was he younger or older than I? Men in grey suits can be deceptive, I thought. He might be younger but still be senior – or older and junior to me. It was a sticky one, this.

'I was here till '51.'

'That's when I came,' he settled the question in good, headmasterly style.

Jack showed me to the William Burrow Library where the man with the bunch of keys and the clutch of wine glasses was now laying out tables for coffee, and to the Principal's old house which was now the Social Club where drinks would later be served at the bar. Heavens! This was where Principal Canon Platten 'cured' his own tobacco leaves in the sun, and dreamed up his sermons and planned the way ahead.

I detached myself from the gathering throng and, seeing it was still early, decided to take a bus into town. Near the Khyber Pass Laundry I mounted a number 55, but could not obtain a ticket without the correct fare. I charged across to Braggs' Bakery where a kind lady gave me every coin imaginable in change for a pound. There were buses every six or seven minutes, she said: 'Feeftee-seeks pence.' Black and red stood the Viaduct and the Gas Works, Nechels, St Matthews Church, as we swung by. They were dwarfed by tower blocks now. Lister Street, Gosta Green, Ansell's, Mitchell's and Butler's; EXPLORE MELBOURNE IN RURAL DERBYSHIRE shouted a hoarding with primary-colour cheer. The Maclaren Building announced itself. So did the Argus Superstore. The General Hospital lay one way, the Citizens Advice Bureau

175

the other. At the Aston Triangle I got off. Corporation Street, the Commercial Union, Rackham's, Smith's lay ahead. H. Samuel's clock said 9 a.m. And there was Cherry Street where I used to buy music. Past New Street, Cannon Street, Needless Alley, I came to the Town Hall. SEVENTH INTERNATIONAL JAZZ FESTIVAL banners swung high. Victoria Regina looked soberly from her statue by the museum. I came to Paradise Street, the forum, Sir Josiah Mason, the University founder, the Hall of Memory, the new Rep and Symphony Hall. Gee! If only my grandfather could have seen this!

Duty – and a shortage of money – propelled me back to College, to *Nulla Sine Sale Salus*. There was Eric (E.N.) Robinson, senior student of our year, Captain of Rugger and useful on the violin. He had already gathered together Norman Hudson, David Howard (looking like John Betjeman in a straw hat), Reg Moon (tuba player), Dennis Oliver, Geoff Sinclair (the walking soccer referee) – but no Finney, no Adcock, no lads from Yorks or Lancs. I had come the farthest, so I felt entitled to appear late.

We set off for St Saviour's Church – a move that would have delighted the old Vice-Principal.

I was dying for a coffee – or even an unprincipalled gin! No luck. We were boxed in. The ex-Bishop of Coventry was going to preach. And who was this? Our old history tutor, the Rev Murray, apologized for being 'dragged out of obscurity, but the vicar of St Saviour's had found himself double-booked. . .' He was a white-haired ghost of his ever-pale self. He sidled through the versicles and we responded mumblingly. The stand-in organist stepped on the odd wrong note in 'Praise My Soul'; the ex-Bishop assured us that we had the Truth (though all about us were new developments, and colleges like ours had dwindled from twenty-eight to seventeen and, of course, ours had been one of the best.) 'Forth in Thy Name O Lord We Go', we sang – and went. Some stayed behind for communion – but not our lot, and by the time we had taken pictures in the rose-lined walk by the church and threaded our way past Islamic gatherings in the street, it was time for lunch. Well, we had a quick half pint at Prinny's Social Club, and then fell to.

It was pure airline fare, cling-film wrapped and you had to skewer your way through the chicken drumsticks with pasty white plastic implements. The wine was undrinkable, but the Right Hon. Denis Howell MP, PC, rose above the drowth and made an excellent brief speech.

And, of course, although the lunch was terrible, the panelling was terrific.

We spent the afternoon around the sun-baked playing field desultorily watching cricket – a match between Stetchford and Mosely Youth. Scargill's shindy at the Gas Works of 1972 seemed light years away.

But shadows fall at eventide. It was sad, for instance, that the chapel next door to the James Chance Memorial Room was closed. It never did have any golden mellowness, no walls leaning out, no bendy spire. It was always grimy with soot. But soot is used as a cleansing agent sometimes; and so, more often, is salt.

The Vice-Principal used to say 'There is more to travel than scenery', and I could not have walked and driven up and down England as I had done in the last two years without beginning to see what he meant. But experience had set up ambivalences, dilemmas even, in my mind. Walking – or driving – I was all right. It was when I

177

tried to decide where I stood that the problems presented themselves. Satisfied though I was that England was a fine place to live, there were many aspects of life in England that left me ill at ease. They were socio-economic, they were political, they were religious and educational. Moreover, they were personal. Did England know where it was going? And – becoming increasingly more urgent with age – did I?

Standing on White Horse Hill, I had been almost conscious of the earth's spinning; and that I, among the restless larks and settled sheep, was an isolated atom not quite rooted in the universe. But that, we know from people who climb real mountains, is the effect that altitude usually has on the human mind and form; it reduces them to insignificance. Returning to the valley, we resume making pictures, selecting views and placing them in pleasing perspectives which tell us less about the views than they do about ourselves.

What, for example, has been the full effect of the sheep – the animal whose hooves 'turn sand to gold' – on English landscape and history? The great wool churches built to the glory of God (and also, one must add, to the glory of the landlords and businessmen who raised them) inspire a sense of awe which leads to a willing suspense of disbelief. The sheep's effect on landscape has been wonderful ... turning the richest parts of the country into National Trust and English Heritage parks which support (after a fashion) stately homes whose tree-studded acres look like lawns. But it is impossible to escape the haunting thought that to accommodate those golden hooves the Enclosures in England and Wales, as much as the Clearances in Scotland, led to the expulsion of people from the land.

That is horrible to contemplate; but against it ... can one regret what it did for the one man who could look after five hundred sheep? The shepherd was not only a farmworker who survived, but he was the man, more than any other, to whom the farmer or landowner turned for advice. He was almost indispensable.

This is well brought out in Sheila Stewart's book *Lifting the Latch* where her friend the Oxfordshire shepherd Mont Abbott says: 'It used to puzzle me how with all his education the boss could only count sheep one at a time, stabbing the air with his forefinger. He'd lose count, flare up, fling his arms about and upset the sheep. I always stood still, holding up my crook, dividing them off in tens in my head.' He could measure whole acres, standing still; tell to within a foot how many rolls of wire would be needed to fence a field; and reckon in his head how long the keep would last, given so many acres, so many sheep and so much a day.

'What did we do last year?' To him – and to many of the cowmen and horsemen of old – it was a simple question. Without a computer or a filing system he would deliver the answer.

'D'ya reckon?'

'Sart'n sure, boss. Sart'n sure.'

But something went wrong with this organic bonding of the rural community: something complex, not easily reckonable in my head.

Straight from my Priory School history notes comes the phrase, 'The Speenhamland System'. Little did I think as a boy that I would ever live near the site of the old Pelican Inn in Newbury where those Justices of the Peace – well-meaning parsons and hard-headed farmers – sat down in 1795 and tried to devise an acceptable (to them) scale of relief for the agricultural poor, based on the price of a quartern loaf of bread – whatever that might be. (Of course the farmers had a vested interest in keeping up the price of bread; even a seventeen-year-old could see that.) Temporary expedient it was meant to be, but accepted it was – and adopted as a general practice over a large part of the land. England's generally admired system of Poor Relief was brought into disrepute. Even after the repeal of the Corn Laws in 1846 the lax attitude of landlords towards their dependants, brought about by that cosy decision in a pub, proved to have far-reaching adverse effects on England's rural poor.

J.L. and Barbara Hammond devote most of their book *The Village Labourer* to the state of the labourer in 1795, the remedies of 1795 and their terrible after effects. No one aged seventeen could read that book and not be deeply affected by it. I quote here only the final paragraph.

De Quincey has compared the blotting out of a colony of Alexander's in the remote and unknown confines of civilisation, to the disappearance of one of those starry bodies which, fixed in longitude and latitude for generations, are one night observed to be missing by some wandering telescope. 'The agonies of a perishing world have been going on, but all is bright and silent in the heavenly host.' So it is with the agonies of the poor.

The Speenhamland System is typical of England's happy-go-lucky, *ad hoc* history. The Englishman prides himself on muddling through. He boasts of an unwritten constitution; a choice of private or state education; an Established Church – but no obligation to use it; a National Health Service; and a legal system which – like the other four – he traditionally regards as 'the envy of the world'. But what has he really got? It might not be too melodramatic to suggest he has a constitution which is being rapidly spelt out to him by Brussels; an education system poorly funded,

180

divided and unstable; a Church of England in decline if not in schism; a National Health Service which is public but no longer free; and a legal system in disrepute.

But then, caution and conscience say, 'Hold it – it might not be so bad as all that.' It may be more important to conserve the bonding of society than to change it – which almost always means loosening it.

In a brief survey, a lightning social overview, let us start at the top: the monarchy seems at odds with itself and the aristocracy has been forced by taxation to set up shop – a very English way out. Both still have popular appeal, and bring in a lot of revenue. (That, to the Englishman, is a telling argument for keeping anything.) No doubt King Alfred or Edward the Confessor would have preferred an aristocracy instituted from within; William the Conqueror imposed one from without. Hence, no doubt, the distrust which the average Englishman feels for it. But he does not exactly dislike it. He may, in fact, secretly envy it.

No, it is not so much the nobs as the middle-class snobs that the common Englishman really dislikes. And there are more and more of them.

Once, our social structure was broadly based on land tenure. Now it is loosely based on money. Land equalled stability. Money equals flux. And its attendant snobbery is the most noxious and socially divisive influence we have to fight against; it results in the unleavening of society and produces a poison of such virulence that it is more corrupting than moth or rust.

Farmers are too earth-bound to be snobs. Rarely, if one is lucky enough to encounter a farmer walking, does he have his head in the air. He is more likely to have his eyes and nose to the ground. He is feasting his eyes on the quality of the tilth, or the turf – the latter reseeded perhaps with a new ley, for 'grass is green gold'. Everything that matters to a farmer is long term. He has to think ahead.

Ugly as many of his buildings may be, he is – beyond the farm yard – the best planner on earth. He it is who has given us our ponds, woodlands and hedges (even if, in an aberration of the sixties, he started filling them in and grubbing them out). He it is who still, like his father before him, looks after his own acres and God's. He is generally, if he lives by the church, grass-cutter, mole-catcher, and churchwarden to boot. If he does not catch the moles himself, he knows someone who can; if he does not actually mow the churchyard, he rigs up a movable fence and turns in some sheep. He is humble enough about his faith ('I'm a very imperfect Christian,' Bill Sinnett told me, snatching up a little black lamb from the roadside and returning it to the field and its mum), but better an imperfect Christian than a know-all Atheist, I say. Farmers are generally rich in sound judgement and practical commonsense.

'Bah! Who cares about books?' said a man called Trajan, who had once been a true knight. 'Not all the learning of the Church could drag me out of hell, but only love and good faith, and my own just judgments.' This memorable explosion on the pages of *Piers Plowman* might have been written with the farmer in mind. Certainly not the man for whom money means all. 'Without charity the Law is not worth a bean!' Trajan goes on. 'And every branch of learning, and all the seven Arts, are a waste of time unless you learn them for the love of God.'

'Live as if you are going to die tomorrow,' is the modern version of that aphorism. 'But farm as if you are going to farm for eternity.'

Left, as it were, on the scrap-heap of society, exposed to every draught that blows from Town Hall or Westminster, are the depressed masses. In the past it was the Church, more than any other institution, that held them in some kind of bonding with the rest of society. And the Farm gave them hope of improving their lot on this earth. But industrial exploitation and economic exigencies combined with a relaxation of moral standards have changed that.

Wilberforce, Owen, Morris, Chadwick, Shaftesbury, Howard and Fry (notably not mainly members of the Church of England) did their damndest in the nineteenth century to rescue the masses from the mire – far more than Engels and Marx, poking around in the sewers of Manchester or scribbling in the library of the British Museum.

It was extraordinary what a wave of piety and good works washed over England in the first half of that century; and how much of it was dissipated in the second. We have to thank the Quakers and Unitarians as well as the Methodists and other free churchmen for what was done. Free thinkers too! The Church of England was too caught up in the Oxford Movement and its own high-minded affairs.

Later, the Salvation Army would come on the scene to provide food, clothing and shelter. And in our own time, the state dishes out benefits, ironically called social security – may yet run a lottery. . . . But the state cannot offer the ultimate Christian blessing: the bond of peace.

When I was seven, at Little Ness Church of England School, I was in command of the Catechism, and could recite from memory the Duty Towards My Neighbour, a code of practice making people answerable not only for their words but also for their deeds. That same year, the Rev F. Brighton, vicar of Great Ness, was rummaging about in the Parish Chest – as was his wont – and drew out an Indenture dated 1719. I quote it as an example of bonding which, in spite of all the opportunities for abuse, must have helped to see our ship of state through the many storms ahead. It is dressed in the language of the Catechism, the Duty Towards My Neighbour in particular.

It begins by stating that the Churchwardens and the Overseers of the Poor of the Parish, by and with the Consent of two of his Majesty's Justices of the Peace – what an assembly! – have put and placed Thomas Bedoe, a poor child of the parish, Apprentice to Richard Whittikars, with him to dwell and serve from the day of this Indenture until the said Apprentice shall accomplish his full Age of four and twenty years ... provided DURING all which term the Apprentice his Master faithfully shall serve in all lawful Business, according to his Power, Wit, and Ability; and honestly, orderly and obediently, in all Things demean and behave himself. ... And the Master will teach and instruct the Apprentice in the business of husbandry ... find, provide and allow meet, competent and sufficient Meat, Drink and Apparel, Lodging and Washing and all other things necessary and fit for an Apprentice ... that he be not a charge upon the Parish ... and at the end of the Term, shall make, provide, allow and deliver unto the Apprentice double Apparel of all Sorts, good and new (that is to say) a good new Suit for the Holy Days, and another for the Working Days.

One suspects that even the wayward Langland would have approved of that – Especially of the Capital Letters.

The book that most surprised me on my trip was the one I picked up in Cleobury Mortimer: *The English Middle Classes* by Roy Lewis and Angus Maude. It was first published in 1949, the year I left Little Ness. Before Lewis and Maude can have their say, however, Aristotle is quoted on the flyleaf, lending his weight to an argument that I was working on and foolishly thought was new.

Great is the good fortune of a state, [the old Greek avows,] in which the citizens have a moderate and sufficient property; for where some possess much, and the others nothing, there may arise an extreme democracy, or a pure oligarchy; or a tyranny may grow out of either extreme – either out of the most rampant democracy, or out of an oligarchy ... and where the middle class is large, there are least likely to be factions and dissensions.

Put more succinctly, in the words of one of my farmer friends, that is: 'We canna be doin' with extremes.'

Lewis and Maude do not decry the English public schools, doubting, they say, whether the 'Public School type still exists'. They argue that there are certain educational benefits that money is still able to buy: social training, the acquisition of the culture of one's peers and superiors, discipline, powers of initiative, self-reliance, poise and a breadth of curriculum which the early specialization in state secondary schools has eaten steadily away. They also call in Squire Brown who, on despatching Tom to Rugby in 1830, sighed hopefully: 'If only he'll turn out a brave, helpful, truth-telling Englishman, and a gentleman, and a Christian, that's all I want.'

Lewis and Maude are very good on that saddest of all modern trends: the loosening of social bonds. They point out that in the seventeenth century England was still mainly agricultural and that, outside the great houses, social distinctions were not very clearly marked. There was a friendly and mutually advantageous relationship between employer and employed which lasted till the Industrial Revolution, after which the newly rich, still insecure, became excessively anxious to fix a gulf between themselves and the lower orders in their households. The rapid population increase of the nineteenth century ensured that there was no shortage of 'damp souls of housemaids' to sprout despondently at area gates. The cheapness of labour

185

(and of life) can be glimpsed in this scale of household staff in relation to income given by Mrs Beeton in 1888:

| Income | Staff |
|---|---|
| £1000 p.a. | cook, two maids, one man |
| £750 | cook, one maid, one man |
| £300 | cook, one maid |
| £200 | one general servant or girl for rough work (the 'slavey', for whom Mrs Beeton gives a terrifying recital of daily tasks) |

I cheered when Lewis and Maude rounded on the too early severance of parental bonds, even at the nursery stage: 'Such children as middle-class parents are foolish enough to have will,' they predict, 'be dumpable in day nurseries and nursery schools.'

They further develop the argument for social bonding in their excellent observations regarding patronage.

'Can the need for charity ever be abolished by social and economic reforms?' they ask. 'In any community worthy the name there will always be individuals able and anxious to help others.' It is not demeaning, they argue; but part of the wholeness of Life with a capital L. It is the virtue so extolled by Langland and St Paul. It is what 'sweetens the giver and recipient in equal measure. It is this Christian charity which is essential to our civilization and which,' they argue, 'we are in danger of losing.'

It is no longer safe to assert that the middle classes, suffering financial schizophrenia, will not demand that public spending be kept to a minimum. Growing numbers of people receive benefits, e.g. University grants. State Santa Claus no longer restricts his gifts to the poor and sick. He will sometimes slip a package down the chimneys of the well-to-do.'

Then, for extra *gravitas*, they bring in J. S. Mill:

186

Every function super-added to Government, causes its influence over hopes and fears to be more widely diffused, and converts more and more the active and ambitious part of the public into hangers-on. . . . If all were in the pay of the Government . . . not all the freedom of the press and popular constitution of the legislature would make this or any other country free otherwise than in name.

Wham!

Finally, I turned to what they have to say about the farmers. 'At a rough estimate there are more than 200,000 farmers in England and Wales who may broadly be described as middle class.' They build up a very clear picture, partly borrowed from my favourite farming historian, Lord Ernle, of an England that changed from the fifteenth-century mainly feudal system of land tenure, through the enclosure of common lands, which went on for a much longer period than is generally supposed, through the disastrous times after Waterloo when 'there was scarcely a solvent farmer left in the Wealds of Kent and Sussex, and many farmers had lost everything and were working on the roads,' then on to the vicissitudes of the nineteenth century at the end of which my grandfather was battling at Red House, Little Ness, against a new Apollyon, the competition from North American wheat.

Still more agreeably, Lewis and Maude go on to extol Richard Jefferies, whose description of a farm sale notice of 1897 in *Hodge and His Masters* is also reminiscent of my years at Little Ness: 'a large white poster, fresh and glaring, is pasted on the wall of a barn that stands beside a narrow country lane. . . .' 'No man drinks the bitter cup of poverty to the dregs like the declining farmer,' he goes on to say. 'The descent is so slow; there is time to drain every drop. . . It may be eight, or ten, or fifteen years. He cannot, like the bankrupt tradesman, even when the fatal notice comes, put up his shutters at once and retire from view.'

187

And now, in 1991, farmers are faced with new diffi-
culties, unexperienced by their fathers and grandfathers
before. 'Farmers, like farming,' our authors say, 'are
changing. The farmer's problem is largely the problem
of the number of hours in a day; for he must be
scientist and technician, businessman and government
clerk. Yet beyond all this he is – and must remain –
a *farmer*. Moreover,' they add, 'farmers and farms are
specialized – in products, even in method, and certainly
in size. Upon this rock the notion, shared by experts
and laymen, that "the small farm is uneconomic" comes
to grief. The success of the small mixed farm, cultivated
intensively by a man who knows what he is doing and is
prepared to work exceedingly hard, simply disproves such
assertions by producing bigger yields per man and per acre
than the highly mechanized large unit.'

Had I read this in 1949 instead of 1991 and had I read
Henderson's classic manual of farm practice *The Farming
Ladder* endorsing the point about hard work – and most
of the organic principles of balanced husbandry in vogue
today – I might have stayed on the farm. As it was, I read
*The Village Labourer* instead. My heart beat to the left. I
was, as I have said, an unbridled colt. And even now, when
I have the harness on and I get the bit between my teeth, I
pull to the left: a natural tendency surely for anyone who
travels, on foot or by car, on the rolling English roads.

# POSTSCRIPT

As I sped home along our newest bit of motorway, delighting in that good-to-be-alive feeling which is the composite effect of freewheeling in a small glass box under a powerful July sun lighting up a world which at this time of the year is most ripe for ravishment, the corn stood high and golden on the Downs. There was even a windmill on top of a hill, its white cap and sails highlighted by the sun. Churches peered out of valleys, clumped with trees; the fields folded one another in their arms, their heads and shoulders swarmed with sheep. Above, the clouds were idle as those painted ships of Coleridge; the sky painted, too. It was nirvana – and only the thought of sudden extinction resulting from a blow-out in the fast lane prevented me being seduced by it.

Slowing down, I wondered where were the cows? The few I had seen were of some Continental breed. And where, in all these fields, were the folk? What, I asked my isolated, insulated self, would Cobbett have made of this? Or Langland? Or the Vice-Principal? The latter would have been happy with the windmill and the sheep. Cobbett probably never saw such corn; but his mind would have detected fraud – some price that had been paid to put on such a show. And Langland would have called Conscience into the debate to confound the C.A.P. All were in favour of Commonsense against the Theorists and Doctrinaires; but even more they liked to see idealism confounding worldly commonsense.

All along this new motorway are signs to lure the gullible motorist to 'Shakespeare Country', or Warwick Castle, or some Cotswold Wildlife Park. The planners have taken the Plain of the world, with its crowded panoramas and ugly close-ups, its noisy comings and goings and its intimate details, and put it up for show in a kind of theatre – exemplified by the Theme Park which

191

Langland and Shakespeare would surely have despised.

But man has always gone in search of the new: New Worlds, New Deals, New Maths, New Breeds, New Potatoes, New Implements, New Washing Powders, New Theories, New Drugs, New Roads to Hell, New Routes to Heaven. . . .

Usually what he thinks new is an old doll in a different dress; or, like the New English Bible, the same story, keeping the sense, but losing the sound. He needs the motorway; but how much more he needs the country lane and – most of all – the path to his back door.

I left the motorway at Chieveley and took the turn for my home village at School Lane. It is one of our Berkshire villages which still retains its school. I should pass Winterbourne church set apart from the village with its companion manor farm and horses nodding under chestnut trees. Cromwell prayed in this church on the eve of the second battle of Newbury. It presents a strong flint face to the surrounding soft cornfields and green wooded hills, the scene of the carnage that followed his prayers.

There is not much set aside on farms round here. Not yet. Sheep rule, OK. But the churches have thin congregations; the folk are dispersed; and the pastor would have a hard job to count up to ninety and nine – not to mention the search for the one that was lost.

It is ironic that just as the world stands in desperate need of physical sustenance, farmers are being urged and tempted to cut production and land is sold or set aside for other purposes; just as the world stands in desperate need of moral and spiritual regeneration, churches are being made redundant, sold or set aside for other purposes, too.

Looking on Winterbourne, with its manor house representing several centuries of aggrandisement, its cottages and farm buildings so familially grouped, the odd thatched cart shed still standing proud among the sunlit brick and tile, I thought of Wordsworth. I felt, like him, 'a sense sublime of something far more deeply interfused, whose dwelling is the light of setting suns'. It is a feeling easily induced at this time of day, at this time of year. Even the flint face of the church seemed to soften and smile. 'The earth is the Lord's and the fulness thereof.' The traveller is impressed by the richness, the roundness, the apparent permanence of things. And I was nearing home. It was consoling, in this world so readily seduced by fashion, to be reminded that before the factory and the film set was the farm; before the Common Market, before Cobbett, Clive or Cromwell, was the church; that they abide, apart, yet side by side.

I returned that evening to the house in Boxford which has been my home for the last ten years; that is half of the time that I spent at Church Farm, Little Ness. Life on the farm was a chiaroscuro of pain and delight which I attempted to describe in two earlier books: *A Corner of Paradise* and *Mare's Milk and Wild Honey*. In *The Farms of Home* I have tried to draw attention to what I believe to be two of our principal national assets, neglected and taken for granted though they often are.

'Work for the Lord: the pay may not be much, but the prospects are out of this world!' You could say the same about working on the land. But now I read that set aside is to become compulsory and lush acres as well as lean will be made waste, if only temporarily. How the weeds will mock and make merry where now the folds are full of sheep and the valleys stand so thick with corn that, as the psalmist says, 'they shall laugh and sing'. Then, no doubt, we shall look as hard for a sheep as we do at present for a man.

Perhaps the Vice-Principal at Saltley foresaw all this.

He who knew the waste of war and was resentful of our youthful, peacetime negligence, may have foreseen that the spectre of want would come back to haunt us on our breakfast plates.

Those who work on the land – and I mean those who really work, not those who regulate or move the money around – are like those who work for the Lord. They bear also a striking resemblance to those who teach. And, rigorous as all three disciplines are, those disciples that are left would wish nothing better than to be allowed freedom and time enthusiastically to do the job.

Retirement is a mixed blessing – it is too much like redundancy – but now that I am about the age that the Vice-Principal was when he made his proposition to me, I do not turn to Cobbett who would have struggled, loudly protesting, against the tide of events – and surely gone under, for he was no better a farmer than I was. I turn to the quiet-voiced intimations of Wordsworth:

> *We will grieve not, rather find*
> *Strength in what remains behind. . .*
>
> *In the faith that looks through death,*
> *In years that bring the philosophic mind.*

# SOURCES OF CHAPTER TITLES

'I take to the open road' from Walt Whitman's *Song of the Open Road*:

*Afoot and light-hearted I take to the open road,*
*Healthy, free, the world before me,*
*The long brown path before me leading wherever I choose.*

———

'On Malvern Hills a marvel befell me' and 'A fair field full of folk' from the prologue to William Langland's *Piers Plowman*:

*In a summer season when the sun was mild*
*I got myself up in a garb as though I'd grown into a sheep;*
*In the habit of a hermit, unholy of works,*
*I went wide in the world, watching for wonders.*
*And on a May morning on Malvern Hills*
*A marvel befell me – magic it seemed.*
*I was weary from wandering and went to rest*
*At the bottom of a broad bank by a brook's side,*
*And as I lay lazily looking in the water*
*I slid into a slumber, it sounded so soothing.*
*Then there came to me reclining there a most curious dream,*
*That I was in a wilderness – where, I'd no idea.*
*But as I looked into the east, up high towards the sun,*
*I saw a tower on a hill-top, trimly constructed,*
*A deep dale beneath, a dungeon-tower in it,*
*With deep dark ditches, dreadful to see.*
*A fair field full of folk I found between the towers,*
*Of people of all positions, the poor and the rich,*
*Working and wandering as the world requires.*

'A Hill called Difficulty': The 'Hill Difficulty' occurs in
John Bunyan's *Pilgrim's Progress*.

I beheld, then, that they all went on till they came to the foot of
the Hill Difficulty; at the bottom of which was a spring. . .

———

'Most roads lead men homewards' from John Masefield's
'Roadways' (with thanks to The Society of Authors as the
literary representative of the Estate of John Masefield):

> *One road leads to London,*
> *One road leads to Wales,*
> *My road leads me seawards*
> *To the white dipping sails.*
>
> *My road calls me, lures me*
> *West, east, south and north;*
> *Most roads lead men homewards,*
> *My road leads me forth. . .*

———

'The farms of home' from the poem of that name by A.E.
Housman:

> *The farms of home lie lost in even,*
> *I see far off the steeple stand;*
> *West and away from here to heaven*
> *Still is the land.*
>
> *There if I go no girl will greet me,*
> *No comrade hollo from the hill,*
> *No dog run down the yard to meet me:*
> *The land is still.*
>
> *The land is still by farm and steeple*
> *And still for me the land may stay:*
> *There I was friends with perished people,*
> *And there lie they.*

197

'Time for amendment' from the Prayer of Absolution (Compline):

May the almighty and merciful Lord grant you pardon and remission of all your sins, time for amendment of life and the grace and comfort of the Holy Spirit.

——

'Forth I wander, forth I must' from the poem of that name by A.E. Housman

> *When green buds hang in the elm like dust*
> *And sprinkle the lime like rain,*
> *Forth I wander, forth I must,*
> *And drink of life again. . .*

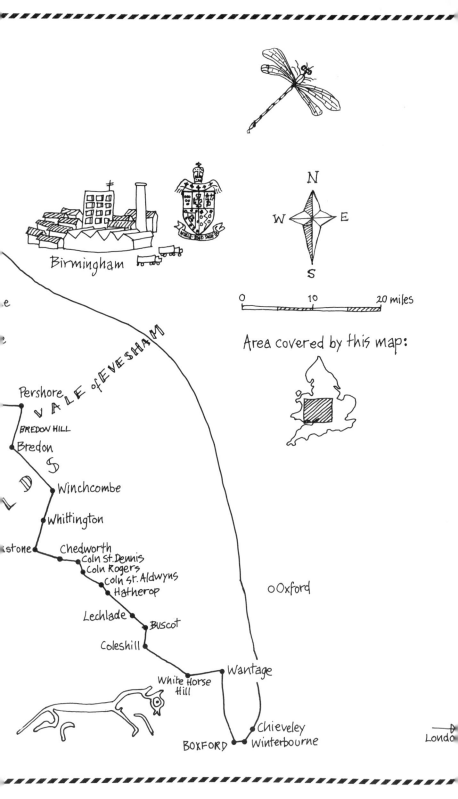

N
W E
S

0   10   20 miles

Area covered by this map:

Birmingham

VALE of EVESHAM

Pershore

BREDON HILL
Bredon

S

Winchcombe

Whittington

Chedworth
Coln St. Dennis
Coln Rogers
Coln St. Aldwyns
Hatherop

Lechlade
BUSCOT

Coleshill

o Oxford

Wantage

White Horse Hill

Chieveley
BOXFORD Winterbourne

Londo